Attractive Thinking

The five questions that drive successful brand strategy and how to answer them

Chris Radford

First published in Great Britain by Practical Inspiration Publishing, 2020

ISBN   978-1-78860-103-0 (print)
        978-1-78860-101-6 (epub)
        978-1-78860-100-9 (mobi)

Practical Inspiration
PUBLISHING

Dedicated to Shona for her unfailing love and support
for me as well as being a mentor, advisor and contributor
to many of the ideas and techniques in this book

Contents

Foreword

Mike Harris

Creator of Iconic Shift mentoring

Founder of First Direct and Egg

Former CEO of Mercury Communications

I have spent a large part of my career creating brands that disrupted the incumbent providers. Each business went on to be sold for significant amounts or created noticeable value for their shareholders reflected in share price, revenue and profit. First Direct was the first telephone bank without branches, Mercury Communications (the Mercury consumer business was ultimately acquired by Virgin Media) was the first challenger to the BT monopoly, Egg was the first internet bank and Garlik (acquired by Experian) provides internet security for everyday people and everyday businesses that goes beyond credit checking, anti-virus software and consumer cyber insurance.

For each of these brands the team worked relentlessly to create a customer experience that was much better than the prevailing norm. We learned that helping customers solve a problem or address a need is the best way to create sustainable growth and to build value for the shareholders.

From these experiences I have drawn some conclusions about what is required to grow a brand that creates shareholder value. This is summed up in some teachable intellectual property I have developed that I call Iconic

Shift. I believe a company wishing to develop a powerful, value-creating brand must pass four tests:

1 A value proposition for their customers that is relevant, distinctive and differentiated.

2 The proposition is communicated with sufficient power and reach.

3 The promised experience is delivered every time, everywhere and every day.

4 The business economics work.

High-growth brands have these four things in place. When growth slows down it is because one or more of these elements is not working as well as it could.

I have worked with Chris. His Attractive Thinking approach and method is the most powerful tool I have come across to help you gain the insight from your customers and turn this into a value proposition for your customers and create the means to communicate it with sufficient power. In my experience many businesses do not pay enough attention to the value they create and offer to their customers. Instead they are focused on how much money they can extract from their customers. Attractive Thinking explains why creating value is better than extracting it and shows you how to do it.

Preface and acknowledgements

I have always held a view that businesses who serve their customers with better products and better service will do better than those that don't. The purpose of business should be to solve a problem for their customer and address their needs. In my world this purpose is ahead of the profit purpose. The reason is not that profit does not matter; it is essential for the business to prosper. But without a customer purpose, the business will not enjoy sustainable profitable growth. This view is not a moral or principled position, but instead is a practical approach to creating a strong brand in a successful business.

When I started business in 1979, I was somewhat surprised to discover that many people did not hold to these priorities. Helping customers solve a problem with products that address their needs is quite often seen as subordinate to achieving short-term profit results. As a result of seeing this reaction from others, for quite a while, I questioned my view that serving customers was the priority and went along with the prevailing views of people around me that short-term results trumped everything. I always campaigned for my way, which was to focus on doing what would attract more customers, but I did not always win the argument.

Over the years with more experience and with more education, studying and research, I have developed my view of what works best. This book, *Attractive Thinking*, is my explanation and analysis of this. It is not just theoretical; it is a practical handbook on how to take this approach.

Part I starts with a rapid tour of the prevailing theory and research on how customers behave, how to attract customers and how to build brands. I will discuss the principles of an approach I call Attractive Thinking and contrast it with Extractive Thinking. In Part II, I then move on to show you a practical five-step framework for building a brand that will attract more customers. This involves answering five questions. The questions are simple but answering them takes graft, creativity and persistence. I also look at research and evidence on how to get to a strategy that everyone is convinced will work. Getting support from everyone for the strategy is hard. I have conducted research into this via my own consultancy, and several academics and the big consultancies have researched and reported on how to win support for a brand strategy. In the final two chapters (8 and 9) I will explore methods and tactics on how to get that engagement.

I hope you will find the book is refreshingly absent of jargon, I have tried to explain things in normal language. It is built on my experience transforming and creating brands with the world's biggest companies such as PepsiCo, Mars, McVitie's, HEAD and Scotts as well as some smaller businesses and high-end business-to-business (B2B) service businesses such as AON Benfield and UL. It covers consumer products, services, leisure and high-end B2B sales.

I will discuss the basics of why people buy and how customers behave. You can use this to develop your own approach that will work in your business and your industry. Every industry needs specialist knowledge. There are specifics and nuances that are important in your industry. You already know what these are. What I would like to do is to shed some light with you on the fundamentals of how customers think and behave and how to attract more of them to your business and brand. Many of these fundamentals are about customers as people and have not really changed, despite the advent of the internet, artificial intelligence, mobile telecommunications and new marketing techniques. I will describe an approach and some principles that work across different business sectors. The fundamentals of how people buy are always about the people who are buying and not the industry that is providing. I will be covering both consumer brands and B2B brands. Now selling to businesses may seem like it is different to selling to consumers. I will argue that the differences are tactical. The principles of creating a strong brand are the same across all sectors. It is still people and individuals who buy, not institutions and organisations.

I am aiming to bring lessons from the world of big business, entrepreneurs and small business and make them accessible to anyone trying to create and manage brands. You do not need big budgets or large teams to take this approach. More money helps but it is not the key to success. The approach is rooted in how people behave and what drives their decisions to buy or not buy.

Attractive Thinking will make your brand and your organisation not just stronger but also 'antifragile'. By answering the five questions in the five steps called PINPOINT, POSITION, PERFECT, PROMOTE and PITCH you can build an organisation and brand that is focused on helping customers solve a problem and address a need. This is dynamic and responsive to customers. Your reputation and ability will be grounded in solving that problem rather than delivering one product or one technology or one service. Your purpose will be to help customers solve that problem. This purpose becomes core to your brand and organisation.

The insights and ideas in this book come from many people and many experiences. They are my take on what matters after working with and listening to many great minds and do-ers in business. I would particularly like to thank the following people for their coaching, encouragement, advice and support on my journey.

For being loyal business partners, fantastic supporters and insightful advisors: Stacey Clark, Henry Schniewind, Shona Radford, Susie Amann, Anna Maxwell, Paul Vines and Simon Tuckey.

For reviewing the first draft and giving me invaluable feedback: Shona Radford, Marcela Flores, Jane Wiley, Mary Grant, James Gambrill, Anne Buckland and Sonya Barker.

For coaching, mentoring and supporting me at work: David Penn, Paul Adams, John Derkach, Ron McEachern, Ross Lovelock, Will Carter, Nick Wright, Martin Hummel, Daniel Priestley, Michael Harris, Andrew Priestley, Phil Martin, Julia Jones, Marion Schofield, John Wyatt, John Postlethwaite, Martyn Wilks, Marylee Sachs, Michael Constantine, Rob Gardner, Jo Rogers, Thao Dang, Guy Tolhurst, Matt Harris, Sue Harris, Suzanne Hazelton, Shireen Smith, Paul Bainsfair, Terry Stannard, Brian Chadbourne, Eric Nicoli, John McDonagh, Simon George, Robert Dodds, Steve Connors, Ian Billington, Helen Stevenson, Tony Mulderry, Arnold Veraart, Alan Pascoe, Sally Hancock, Allyson Binnie, Alain Mahaux, Matthew Taylor, Brian Markovitz, John Jagger, Tony Hillyer, Andy Williams, Patricia Bartlett, Steve Bolton, Steve Acklam, John Scriven, Alan McWalter, Tom Rundle, Wayne Mailloux, Tony McGrath, Andy Neal, Phil Barden, Mark Sugden, Robert Shaw, Nick Wright, David Booth, Rob Taylor, Andrew Easdale and Bridget Cassey.

For being amazing clients and supporters who were fun to work with and taught me at least as much as I helped them: Michelle Frost, Roula Kamhawi, Martin Breddy, Michelle Quickfall, Michael Meinhardt, Dirk Geyer, Keith Stevens, Norman Comfort, Jonathan Garner, John Hassan, Andy Roan, Omar Salim, Ziad Kaddoura, Azhar Malik, Geoff Bryant, Carol Savage, Chris Haskins, Michael Suter, Emma Carter, Brian Moreton, Rachel Collinson, Mark Doorbar, John Postlethwaite, Mark Davis, John Karakadas, Caroline Rudd, Jane Noblet, John Sandom, Mary Say, Michelle Edgington, Stuart Prime, Craig Sherwin, Chris Guy, Leigh Ashton, Jonathan Mills, Suzannah Bartlett, Anthony Newman, Alison Wheaton and Rob Stewart.

And a special thank you to Alison Jones and the Practical Inspiration team for guiding me in the process of writing and producing this book.

Introduction

What is Attractive Thinking and why does it work?

How can Attractive Thinking help you?

What is the purpose of creating or running a business? 'To make money' might be the first thought that comes into our minds. There is no doubt that this features prominently in the minds of people in business and many customers and suppliers will assume the business exists to do that. But is that all there is to it?

'Making a profit' is a subject that preoccupies us as business people. We know that if we don't make a profit, eventually we will not have a business. The Mars chocolate company mentions profit as a part of one of its five principles. The five principles are: Quality, Responsibility, Mutuality, Efficiency and Freedom. But the way they explain freedom is interesting:

> *FREEDOM: We need freedom to shape our future; we need profit to remain free.*

This talks about the function of profit in the business. Profit is about retaining freedom to run the business in the way the family and the management wish to.

Many other people have argued that if a business only exists to make money then something is missing. Businesses are actually about people, customers, staff, shareholders, managers, suppliers. Whilst people need money and we are motivated by money that is not what really drives us. People are about people, their social relations, their dreams, their visions, family, bonds, society and nationality. When businesses ignore this then they do not perform as well as those who recognise it.

Jim Collins and Jerry Porras, in their 1994 classic *Built to Last,* examined the performance of two different types of businesses.[1] They identified firms that were guided by long-term aims and expressed vision and purpose and those managed for short-term profit and shareholder returns. They found that between 1926 and 1990 a group of 'visionary' companies – those guided by a purpose beyond making money – returned six times more to shareholders than explicitly profit-driven rivals.

In 2016 a team from Harvard Business Review Analytics and EY's Beacon Institute conducted research amongst 431 senior executives and published a paper titled 'The Business Case for Purpose', which concluded that those companies able to harness the power of purpose to drive performance and profitability enjoy a distinct competitive advantage.[2]

'Maximising shareholder value' is another often-quoted soundbite. This was very fashionable in the 1980s in business circles. It is still a view that prevails. As recent as 2017 the *Economist*[3] said that the goal of maximising shareholder value is 'the biggest idea in business'. Today 'shareholder value rules business'. The idea of maximising the value and the returns for the owners and investors in the business has an appealing logic. After all, the purpose of investment is to generate a return on the investment. This return arises either from an increased valuation of an asset such as share price, or the health of the balance sheet or the sales, revenue and profit. The original proponents of maximising shareholder value argued that this should

---

[1] James C. Collins and Jerry I. Porras (1994) *Built to Last: Successful Habits of Visionary Companies*, Random House.

[2] Harvard Business Review Analytics Services report, 2016 https://hbr.org/resources/pdfs/comm/ey/19392HBRReportEY.pdf

[3] *Economist*, 31 March 2016 www.economist.com/business/2016/03/31/analyse-this

be the goal of CEOs and the board. This ensures the aims of the CEO and board are aligned with the objectives and expectations of the shareholders.

But in the past 20 years the idea of maximising shareholder value as a goal of business has been increasingly attacked. This includes several high-profile CEOs:

- John Mackey, CEO of Whole Foods, condemned businesses that view their purpose as profit maximisation and treat all participants in the system as means to that end.[4]

- Marc Benioff, Chairman and CEO of Salesforce, declared that this still-pervasive business theory is 'wrong. The business of business isn't just about creating profits for shareholders – it's also about improving the state of the world and driving stakeholder value.'[5]

- Alibaba CEO Jack Ma declared that customers are number one; employees are number two and shareholders are number three.[6]

- Paul Polman, CEO of Unilever, denounced 'the cult of shareholder value'.[7]

---

[4] John Mackey's blog, 28 September 2005 www.wholefoodsmarket.com/blog/john-mackeys-blog/rethinking-social-responsibility-of%C2%A0business

[5] Forbes, 5 February 2015 www.forbes.com/sites/stevedenning/2015/02/05/salesforce-ceo-slams-the-worlds-dumbest-idea-maximizing-shareholder-value/

[6] CBS News, 28 September 2014 www.cbsnews.com/news/alibaba-chairman-jack-ma-brings-company-to-america/

[7] *Economist*, 22 April 2010 www.economist.com/node/15954434/all-comments?page=1

- Larry Fink, the CEO of BlackRock, the world's largest institutional investor, has written to all the CEOs of the S&P 500 and called on them to present long-term strategies. Companies are under-investing in innovation, skilled work-forces or essential capital expenditures.[8]

If we want to understand the arguments that these CEOs put forward, it is helpful to distinguish between means and ends. For Larry Fink, having a business purpose that goes beyond profit is the means to achieve long-term profitable growth and increase shareholder value. The argument runs that if a business focuses on maximising short-term shareholder value it will be less successful at doing this than a business that has a purpose and recognises it must invest in and reward all stakeholders (staff, suppliers, customers, shareholders). In other words, maximising shareholder value is held up as the primary aim of the business, but that the means to achieve that is to focus on a wider set of aims and ensure the business has a purpose that people can get behind.

For John Mackey of Whole Foods, the business purpose beyond profit is the means and the end. His business is all about bringing better food at fair prices and treating suppliers well. The profit and shareholder value are a by-product of that work.[9]

But whether they make purpose the means or the end, more CEOs now agree that having a purpose beyond profit

---

[8] Larry Fink's Chairman's Letter to Shareholders from BlackRock's 2018 Annual Report www.blackrock.com/corporate/investor-relations/larry-fink-chairmans-letter

[9] John Mackey (2014) *Conscious Capitalism*, Harvard Business Review Press.

is necessary to create competitive advantage and deliver long-term profitable growth and value to shareholders. This idea works because a business thrives by engaging with all its stakeholders including staff, suppliers, customers, shareholders and its relationship with the public at large. In the Harvard Business Review Analytics and EY Beacon Institute study in 2016 over 80% of the executives interviewed agreed with the following statements:[10]

> *An organisation with shared purpose will have employee satisfaction.*
> *I'm more likely to recommend a company with strong purpose to others.*
> *Our business transformation efforts will have greater success if integrated with purpose.*
> *An organisation that has shared purpose will be more successful in transformation efforts.*
> *Purpose-driven firms deliver higher-quality products/services.*
> *An organisation with shared purpose will have greater customer loyalty.*

Marketers and CEOs have been swept up in the discussion of purpose and have tried to 'borrow' a purpose and attach it to their business. This can easily backfire if the purpose does not seem to have much to do with the company (Figure 0.1).

---

[10] Harvard Business Review Analytics Services report, 2016 https://hbr.org/resources/pdfs/comm/ey/19392HBRReportEY.pdf

Figure 0.1 Source: Marketoonist.com

In 2018 Lush Cosmetic stores attached themselves to an emerging story about undercover police officers in the Metropolitan Police engaging in deceitful romantic liaisons. There was a public backlash as to why a store selling bath bombs was getting involved. Lush got profile and awareness by doing this, but it did seem unconnected to their brand.

Gillette launched a purpose campaign that was about men having respect for women. This came under criticism for the observation that Gillette did not entirely live up to this themselves, particularly for charging women higher prices for the same razors as used by men.

In 2017 Omar Rodríguez Vilá and Sundar Bharadwaj wrote in the *Harvard Business Review* about brands trying to adopt a social purpose that is only slightly related to their core business:[11]

---

[11] Omar Rodríguez Vilá and Sundar Bharadwaj, *Harvard Business Review*, September 2017 https://hbr.org/2017/09/competing-on-social-purpose

Managers often have the best intentions when trying to link their brands with a social need but choosing the right one can be difficult and risky and has long-term implications. Competing on social purpose requires managers to create value for all stakeholders—customers, the company, shareholders, and society at large—merging strategic acts of generosity with the diligent pursuit of brand goals.

So, some business leaders recognise that expressing a purpose that goes beyond profit and embraces customers, staff, suppliers and shareholders can also maximise long-term financial returns. More recently, creating and communicating a purpose beyond profit has almost become a fashionable pursuit amongst business leaders and marketers. Some businesses have come unstuck when they adopted a purpose that is not the core of what they do. Some businesses have also been criticised for focusing too much on social purpose and that this has been at the expense of short-term profits. Where does this leave us as business owners and leaders who want to attract more customers and create a sustainable long-term business? We like having a purpose in our business; we kind of know that business is about more than profit. But we also know that businesses are about profitable growth and creating shareholder value.

In this book you will get to discover an approach to brand building and business growth that I call Attractive Thinking. Attractive Thinking is a method to attract more customers, motivate more staff, collaborate with more suppliers and reward more shareholders. This approach resolves the questions about how business purpose, shareholder value, growth and profit are connected. It delivers a platform to create, build and grow our brands.

It is built on the belief that our business will only really prosper if we embrace all the stakeholders. In particular, we must attract and embrace customers, shareholders, staff and suppliers. If we can attract and motivate more of each of these critical groups of people, then we will be more successful.

Creating a business purpose that works

The idea of business purpose has been around for a long time. Back in 1954, Peter Drucker chose to keep it simple and offered a simpler yet profound definition of business purpose: 'to create a customer'. Drucker wrote:[12]

> It is the customer who determines what a business is. For it is the customer, and he alone, who through being willing to pay for a good or for a service, converts economic resources into wealth, things into goods. What the business thinks it produces is not of first importance – especially not to the future of the business and to its success. What the customer thinks he is buying, what he considers 'value', is decisive.

This powerful thought seems to have been lost in the current debate around purpose, profit and shareholder value. Yet this simple definition underpins Attractive Thinking. For me, this simple idea resolves the issues raised in the debate around purpose and profit. This definition crystallises the most important thing that a business must focus on: The customer. Drucker's definition connects

---

[12] Peter Drucker (2007) *The Practice of Management*, Routledge.

several important themes in a business. The Attractive Thinking approach builds on this. *The purpose of business is to solve a customer problem and address a need.* When purpose is framed liked this, then it is apparent that our business purpose is our core activity, not a nice to do 'add on'.

In Part I, I will examine research and evidence about how customers think and behave to understand why this works. In Part II, I will show a practical framework that will help ensure our business

- gets more customers so we can grow;

- delivers value for money so that people will come back for more;

- creates growth so we can survive and prosper;

- delivers a profit today, tomorrow, next year and beyond;

- manages costs so we deliver profitable growth;

- motivates the team to deliver more, innovate and drive productivity;

- makes this a fun place to work;

- attracts staff so we can do all the above.

Attractive Thinking drives a much better focus and much better decisions than just setting out to maximise shareholder value. Attractive Thinking helps you to take the idea that we exist to *create a customer* and translate that into a sustainable profitable business in both the short term and the long term.

The role of marketing and the CEO

The responsibility for driving a customer-first or customer-led agenda and setting out the purpose of the business rests firmly with the CEO. But often the CEO needs a team to support them in doing that. The Marketing Society in the UK asserts that this is the job of marketing. Marketing is not just there to produce the websites, the brochures, run the exhibitions and manage the advertising. In the most successful businesses, the marketing function sees itself in the role envisaged by Drucker:

to create a customer

The Marketing Society[13] states that the job of marketers is 'to create sustainable growth by understanding, anticipating and satisfying customer need'. This is the function of marketers, the CEO and business owner/managers. The CEO is the lead marketer in any business, he or she does have other jobs, but being lead marketer is one of them. And the Marketing Society then goes on to explain the task of the marketer and say that creating sustainable growth requires marketers and CEOs to focus on three things:

1   Define your future vision of how the organisation will succeed.

2   Engage and inspire the organisation to be customer led.

3   Deliver by creating value for customers.

---

[13]   The Marketing Society Manifesto for Marketing, 2014 www.mark etingsociety.com/

Figure 0.2 from the Marketing Society explains how this works to create sustainable growth.[14] This is quite different from how marketing is seen and talked about in many businesses. Marketing is often thought of as the function that does the advertising, produces the brochures, the website, runs the promotions and maybe handles any market research.

Figure 0.2 Source: The Marketing Society, June 2019

This definition makes marketing more central and fuses the role of the marketing function with the CEO. Marketers must 'understand, anticipate and satisfy customer needs'. This underpins the Attractive Thinking approach.

However, there is some way to go to make this happen in all organisations. At the time of writing this chapter,

---

[14] The Marketing Society Manifesto for Better Marketing Leadership, 2019

Marketing Week[15] published an article reporting on new research by Dentsu Aegis Network. They reported: 'According to research by Dentsu Aegis, just 25% of UK marketers identify "leading disruptive innovation" as a core functional priority'. This suggests that only one-quarter of marketers agree with the Marketing Society view that marketing is not just about marketing communications but is responsible for creating value, creating growth and driving the customer agenda throughout the business.

Attractive Thinking believes it is important that the CEO and the marketers are not just charged with maximising sales and profits from what we make and sell today, but are also responsible for deciding what we produce, deliver and sell in the future. The Attractive Thinking principle is that to attract more customers, we must understand what they want now, anticipate what they will want in the future and then ensure we produce and deliver it.

What you will get from this book

You will learn about an Attractive Thinking approach that makes the job of creating a customer a lot easier.

In Part I we will explore why Attractive Thinking works. We look at why attracting more customers is better than extracting more profit from the customers we already have. We will explore fundamental principles that work for both consumer and B2B brands. This is split into three chapters.

---

[15] Marketing Week, 31 July 2018 www.marketingweek.com/2018/07/31/uk-marketers-falling-behind-innovation/

In Chapter 1, we examine why we must always start with the customer and how to do this in our business and what might stop us. This begins with setting out that our business purpose is to solve a problem and address a need that our customers have.

In Chapter 2, we will look at how to understand customers, how market research can help us and where it does not help us, and when we need to find alternatives. We will study some universal rules of customer behaviour that must guide our brand strategy and marketing plans.

In Chapter 3, we will look at why it is so difficult to get this right and a few pitfalls where we might stumble and challenges we must overcome. This includes the role of unconscious biases, the influence of randomness and unexpected events, the hazards of trying to predict the future, and why we must be wary of common sense and conventional wisdom and instead look at science and empirical evidence.

This sets up the idea that we need to make our businesses 'antifragile'. This means our business is not just robust but is also dynamic and able to thrive on unexpected shocks.

In Part II, we look at how to apply the Attractive Thinking method. This is a five-step process to create a brand that will attract more customers and not just extract profit from existing customers. We will avoid marketing jargon. Each step has a name and creates the answer to a question:

1   PINPOINT – Who are our customers and what are their problems?

2   POSITION – How can we solve their problems and stand out?

3   PERFECT – How do we create a product, service or message that delivers this?

4   PROMOTE – How do customers find out about it and where do they buy it?

5   PITCH – How do we engage our shareholders, board directors, colleagues and customers?

At the end you will have a brand strategy that everyone is convinced will work. Throughout this book, I want to work with you. I will adopt the approach that we are embarking on this voyage of discovery and planning together.

Part I
Why does Attractive Thinking work?

Chapter 1

Start with the customer

Something strange happens to people when they cross the doorway into their workplace. We all have this blind spot. We spend much of our non-work time acting as a customer and thinking like a customer. We see businesses through the viewpoint of the customer. But as soon as we enter our workplace, we lose that perspective and start thinking like a supplier. We all need to work hard to combat this and look at things from the customer's point of view. Great business leaders can do this persistently and with ease, but they are rare. The rest of us need to work at it. There are two aspects to this to look out for.

Understand what really matters to customers

The supplier (that is us, the marketers and creators) will often misjudge what is important to customers about the product or service. For example, when a hotel manager and conference organiser for a big conference are asked about how they organise the coffee breaks at a big event and what really matters to the conference guests, the manager comes up with a list like this:

- great tasting coffee;
- clean crockery;

- nice buns, snacks and biscuits;
- immaculate table linen;
- smiling helpful staff.

This list describes things that do matter. But when you ask the guests what matters to them, they have different priorities. Their list is like this:

- high-capacity washrooms so I don't have to queue;
- fast access to tea and coffee;
- drinks other than tea and coffee;
- lots of space to hang out with people;
- somewhere to make a quick phone call.

The customer list is not about the features of the coffee and catering service. It is about whether I can do what I want to do in the coffee break. We can have no doubt the items in the manager's list do matter to the conference guests. But the chances are they take these catering things for granted. The guest's list is about things that if they are not in place, then the experience is frustrating. The customer list shows us things where we could be exceptional.

The ability to focus on benefits that matter rather than features that don't

In my consulting business Differentiate, when we do the work in POSITION, we ask our clients to determine the features and benefits that will attract customers. They generate a list and a ranking. We then ask the customers to come up with their list and ranking. The management team usually get about an 80% match with the customer view. Most typically the difference is that the management are convinced that things that are difficult to do or expensive to produce are valuable for the customers. But the problem is the customer places no value on our investment and hard work. They only value things that help them achieve something or experience something that they desire and value.

Here is an example where we asked conveyancing lawyers what mattered to their customers in choosing a conveyancing firm to complete their house purchase or sale. Here are their top seven features and benefits of their service that matter to customers. The emphasis in this list is based on their competence and hard work:

Conveyancing lawyers' list of what is important (is what they do)

1   Service consistently good.

2   Will get deal done quickly.

3   Has good admin back-up.

4   Has experience and knowledge.

5   Works hard on my behalf.

6   Proficient at conveyancing.

7   Can rely on info they give.

These are all important and worthy attributes. But when we asked the customers, the emphasis was different. The customers are after getting the deal done, being updated and a proactive approach. What they care about is the outcome:

Conveyancing customer list of what is important (is the results they achieve and experience they have)

1   Will get deal done quickly.

2   Foresees and solves problems.

3   Keeps me updated.

4   Calls back quickly.

5   Answers phone quickly.

6   Takes responsibility and is proactive.

7   Service consistently good.

If we want to start with the customer, we must shake off the supplier's mindset and get a customer's mindset. We will look at how to do this in detail in PINPOINT and POSITION.

Now we will explore why starting with the customer is so fundamental to growing our brand, the four things all successful businesses have in place, some examples of successful businesses and the four insights about customers that we must understand.

High-growth businesses have four things in place

Have you noticed that when things are going well for a business everything seems to fall into place? Customers turn up, they buy the products, staff want to come and work for the firm, the business has spare cash, people are having fun at work. It feels like that growth will continue forever.

As an example, Daniel Priestley's Dent company runs a programme called Key Person of Influence for entrepreneurs who want to raise their profile and accelerate their growth. The way Dent runs their business makes it look easy. They promote their scorecard with advertising, they have a lot of free content, they run events which seem to fill up easily, people who come to the events sign up for their strategy sessions and their Key Person of Influence course programmes are full.

On a different scale, Google appears to effortlessly attract a higher share of advertising £s $s and €s each year. Google seems to find it easy to be the most popular search engine with the most users.

Big food brands such as Marmite, Kellogg's, Coca-Cola, Walkers, Danone and Wall's Ice Cream make it appear they don't have to sell their products, they just put their products on the supermarket shelf and people buy them, the brands seem to sell themselves.

To the outsider or the competitor, it seems these successful players have secured a position that gives them an unassailable advantage. Smaller competitors feel like they must work harder to get the same results. To some extent it is true that these successful businesses have secured an advantage. But what we can be sure of is that it did not and does not just fall into their laps. They may make it look easy but it is not easy; these businesses work relentlessly to ensure they have four things in place:

1 A value proposition for their customers that is relevant, distinctive and differentiated.

2   They communicate it with sufficient power.

3   They make sure they deliver it every time and every day.

4   The business has basic economics that work.

These four success factors for business were shown to me by Mike Harris[16] during a training and mentoring session and when I saw them it was like a bolt from the blue. There is not really anything else that you need to do to create business success. High-growth businesses have all these four things working together. Businesses that struggle are missing one or two of them or are just a bit weak on one or two of them.

I can hear you thinking, there is another success factor Chris has not mentioned. What about people? A well-motivated, professionally managed and skilled workforce is perhaps the most important factor for success. This is true. Without a great team, we cannot create success. But what we are examining in this book is what the team is setting out to achieve. I will leave other books to examine the skills of leadership, recruitment and team motivation. Attractive Thinking is all about what our team needs to do to attract more customers. Let's examine each of these four success factors.

A value proposition for customers that is relevant, distinctive and differentiated

Our value proposition is what we do for or will offer to our customers that will make them willing to offer us a

---

[16] Mike Harris, Founder and CEO of First Direct, Egg Bank and Garlik.

payment. If we are selling textiles to garment makers that might be some functional things such as the fabric, the quality, the colours, patterns, the quantity, the delivery timing. It might also be some emotional things such as the brand name, the presentation and logo, the sales relationship, the previous experience of our service.

If like Dent we are selling a training course, it could be the business results I could expect, the networking and people I will meet, the track record of the trainers, the number of hours of training, the training materials. It will certainly be some emotional stuff about how I feel towards the trainers and the people I meet and see around me.

If it is food brands then taste, quantity, packaging, convenience, availability when I need it, how well it fits with my needs or meal occasions. There are also important emotional responses to how the experience of the food and the brand makes us feel. Brand reputation, packaging style, brand name, logo, what my friends and family think, perceptions of quality and fitting in with my lifestyle all matter.

The things described so far make the value proposition relevant to the customer. They ensure we design a product or service that answers our customer's need. But relevance is only the base line for getting started. The successful business needs to go further and be distinctive and differentiated. By distinctive, I mean capable of being recognised and noticed and understood. So, for food brands that is usually a combination of great visibility and availability in lots of shops and sometimes topped up with TV or other media advertising and sponsorship. It also includes packaging, naming and descriptions that attract customers and make it clear what it is. By differentiated, I mean just how many other people offer the same as we do. In what way is our product different and distinctive?

So, for example, just how many people offer entrepreneur training targeting the same need to the same people that Dent do? What is it that makes the Dent offer stand out? In their case, it is a whole mix of things. The network their clients get to meet, the success track record of the trainers, the intellectual property (IP) in the way they explain their tools and methods, the way they run their workshops, the way they run their sales process.

In many markets the opportunity to differentiate is much harder. In food brands there are so many me too products and brands with marginal differences. Think about yoghurts, orange juice, biscuits, soft drinks, chocolate bars. The leading brands end up focusing on being available in more places and using their superior marketing budgets to create awareness and recognition in the customer's mind and invest in visibility in the shops.

We will explore the whole subject of creating value propositions that are relevant, distinctive and differentiated in PINPOINT and POSITION.

Communicate with sufficient power

As we get into the 'How to do it' section of this book in Part II, we will learn that the Attractive Thinking approach to brand strategy and business growth is simple. What we must do is to create a product or service that solves a customer's problem. Once we have done that, we need to let them know about it. When the customer discovers our offer, provided we have perfectly solved their problem, they will buy it. We do not need manipulative marketing methods and do not need to trap people into buying things they don't need. We just need to let them know about it and make it easy to buy.

When I worked in big food brands, I did not really understand how simple this is. We were always under pressure to shift more product. The factory was making it, we needed to sell it. Now this pressure to keep the factory busy and sell is real, essential and perfectly proper for a food-manufacturing business. But in the midst of this we would forget that it would be easier to sell what the customer wants than what we have already got.

This became much clearer to me when I started selling consulting services to marketing directors and CEOs. I tried all sorts of means to persuade them that they needed the Differentiate brand strategy process and this included all the usual techniques of advertising, direct mail, telephone sales, speaking at conferences, getting trade press coverage and writing articles. But one day it dawned on me that the only time we ever got any business was when a client prospect called us. It was never when we called them. When we called them, they were busy and preoccupied with other things. When they called us, they wanted to talk to us about a project where they needed some help. Their need had arisen, they had a problem they needed to solve and we could discuss it.

The clear lesson from this was that we had to concentrate on a process that led to them calling us when they needed us. What did that mean? It meant researching what the client's biggest problems were that we could help them with. Then designing a service that addressed these problems and then finding ways to let them know about it and keep reminding them that we existed so that when the time was right for them, they called us.

This is the Attractive Thinking approach to 'communicate with sufficient power'. For the Attractive Thinker, this just means let enough people know about what we offer as frequently as possible, so that when they need it, they remember we have the solution and are able to get hold of us or our product and then buy it.

Those successful businesses I mentioned earlier all have significant budgets attached to letting people know about it and making it easy to buy. Dent advertises and promotes its scorecard and brand accelerators as in-store 'product for prospects' and uses telephone sales to follow up leads. Food brands use advertising in TV, print, outdoor, digital and sponsored events to keep in the consumer's mind and use in-store merchandising and promotional activity to draw attention to their products in store or online. Litmans (a lace and fabric supplier to the garment trade) attends the major trade shows to get buyers' attention as well as some limited advertising. This is followed up by telephone sales and appointments.

In PROMOTE, we will explore how we come up with a budget and get this right for our businesses.

Making sure we deliver it every time and every day

This is a simple idea but hard to do. When we satisfy customers and make them happy, customers tell others about it and they come back and buy again. If we fail to deliver the quality or the service and the customer is frustrated, then we run the risk of losing them as they start to consider alternatives.

In food brands there can be a tussle between the commercial need to hit annual targets and the marketers' desire to protect the reputation and quality of the brand. Small 'adjustments' to product specification will improve profit margins and create an instant rise in profits. If we do this once no-one notices, but if we do this several times the reduction in quality starts to show. Version

2 may be similar to version 1, version 3 very similar to version 2, version 4 very similar to version 3, but version 4 ends up quite different from version 1. Some big food manufacturers have been doing these product tweaks or 'value engineering' for decades.

This has opened up the opportunity for niche quality food suppliers and new brands. The opening for these has often been created by quality reductions amongst the big brands. For example, Ben and Jerry's ice cream and more niche companies such as Purbeck Ice Cream have changed ice cream markets. The bread and baking business has enjoyed a resurgence away from the big bakeries of Hovis and Mother's Pride in favour of handmade artisanal and sourdough breads.

In contrast, Mars, who are the world's biggest private chocolate maker, have stuck to their guns on product quality. This is partly because they are a family-owned business and the family have chosen to protect product quality rather than inflate short-term profits. They continue to quietly grow sales even in their mature markets and consumers still regularly trust and buy their products. Unfortunately, the same cannot be said for some other chocolate manufacturers who have been financially engineering products and moving manufacturing to new locations (in food, location affects product quality). This has opened the door for quality providers such as Lindt to move in and pick up more of their customers.

Similar things happen in other industries. In service industries, we put in fewer hours or miss a deadline and the client notices, or we put on cheaper junior staff to support the project. In tech, the support for when things go wrong is not there; the customer cannot get an answer and drifts away.

In PERFECT, we will explore how we design products that work for customers.

The business has basic economics that work

Whether or not profit is the primary purpose of your business, if it does not make a profit (or persuade investors that its asset price will grow in the future e.g. Uber, Airbnb, Amazon, Google, Facebook) then it will not survive. We need cash and profit to pay for the previous three success factors. This is the fourth success factor. It really boils down to two measures:

Profit – does it cost more or less than the customer is willing to pay to deliver the product and service the customer wants?

Cashflow – will the business have enough cash to do everything it needs to do, or will it run out of money? If the business cannot support its early cash requirements, then are there options to secure loans or investor equity capital to see it through the development period?

As marketers and creators, we need to run the numbers and track performance. If we create a business plan and have that verified with our team and a finance professional, then we can get on with building a brand and invest in that as long as we track:

- sales volumes;
- sales revenues;
- pricing;
- cost of goods;
- overhead expenses;

- working capital;
- speed of payment by customers.

If we have these under control, then the profit and cashflow will follow. We need to understand this. Financial control is an important subject that is a whole separate discipline that we will not be covering in this book.

Who is responsible for each of the four things you must have in place?

Have a think about who looks after each of these four things in your business:

1   A value proposition for their customers that is relevant, distinctive and differentiated – who does this?

2   Communicate it with sufficient power – usually sales and marketing.

3   They make sure they deliver it every time and every day – usually operations, technical, customer service.

4   The business has basic economics that work – usually finance.

Many businesses do not have a function that is dedicated to creating and managing the value proposition. In consumer products branded businesses, the marketers assume responsibility for it. But often it is spread across different functions and the CEO is the only person who manages it. The CEO has many other things to do and needs some help.

Summary of the four things we must have in place

If things are not going too well and our competitors are doing better, then identify which of these four success factors are the problem:

1 A value proposition for their customers that is relevant, distinctive and differentiated.

2 They communicate it with sufficient power.

3 They make sure they deliver it every time and every day.

4 The business has basic economics that work.

One of the ways to fix number 1 is to reduce the price, but that messes up number 4. We may have to do that in the short term to survive. But we really need to fix the value proposition. In Part II, PINPOINT, POSITION, PERFECT and PROMOTE reveal the Attractive Thinking way to do this.

Attracting vs extracting

As a business leader we are driven by numbers, especially financial ones. These could be a matter of survival (cashflow), growth targets (revenue), generating returns (profit), or controlling costs (profit). We need profit as a means to retain freedom and control over the destiny and direction of the firm. The financial success of a business is a function of some critical numbers:

1 Prospects – the number of prospective customers.

2 Customers – the number of prospects who buy.

3   Volume – the number of sales made.

4   Price – the price achieved on each sale.

5   Revenue – which is volume {multi} price.

6   Costs – how much it costs to make each sale.

7   Overheads – the permanent infrastructure cost to run the business: Labour, premises, IT.

8   Profit – which is revenue less costs and overheads.

9   Capital invested – how much money has been spent to set up the business.

10 Working capital – how much money is tied up in the business e.g. stock or unpaid invoices.

11 Cash in the bank – and future cashflow.

12 Assets – things that we own that will produce income e.g. property, IP, machinery, systems, processes, customer lists, distribution agreements, franchisees, brand reputation.

13 Return on assets/capital – which is the ratio of profit to capital and working capital.

14 Share price or shareholder value – our current numbers plus the shareholders' view of the prospect of us improving these numbers in the future.

That is a lot to keep an eye on, so we need to establish priorities. I find that if we focus on the number of customers, the price achieved, the cost of goods/services and make sure we collect on invoices promptly, the rest of the numbers fall into place. But it will be different for each business and for different business leaders.

Which numbers are the right ones to focus on? This depends on our situation. It will also be influenced by our need for quick wins and immediate gains vs our desire to create sustainable longer term growth or profit. Remember Collins and Porras in *Built to Last*[17] produced some convincing evidence that purely focusing on the short term will not be as successful in the long term vs an organisation that invests in the future and knows its purpose.

How to choose the numbers you should prioritise?

There is one overarching factor that will determine how we make decisions, and this is whether we are focused on attracting more customers or extracting the most profit from our existing customers. This is also related to whether we are after quick wins and short-term gains in profit or want to build a long-term sustainable business. This mindset will drive the priorities and your decision making.

Attractive Thinking is about building a long-term sustainable business whilst also getting quick wins and short-term profits. It does not accept that there is a choice between the long term and the short term. What we must do is make our offer to customers more valuable and more visible and more available so we will attract more customers. Whereas the extractive approach is about the quickest and easiest way to maximise short-term gains.

---

[17] James C. Collins and Jerry I. Porras (1994) *Built To Last: Successful Habits of Visionary Companies*, Random House.

Let's look at some examples of Attractive Thinking and the extractive approach.

The extractive approach is summed up by Figure 1.1. The extractive mindset looks at customers in much the same way as the cowboy here with his lasso. The customer is there to be targeted and captured, or even trapped into buying our stuff and preferably more stuff than they need. The customer is our victim. This is how customers sometimes feel when trapped by deals and offers. A good example is mobile phone contracts that force us to pay for more than we need each month; insurance companies that silently increase prices to people who renew their policy without shopping around; banks coming up with ever more hidden ways to charge customers whilst pretending to offer free banking, whilst knowing that we will find any excuse to avoid switching banks. These behaviours of entrapment may then be coupled with a drive to reduce the costs of servicing customers to the point where the customer experience is compromised, and it becomes difficult and stressful for customers to deal with the organisation.

Figure 1.1 Source: 123rf.com; copyright Svetlana Alyuk

Once it is stressful to deal with organisations (think of call centres for banks/phone/broadband) then customers don't really want to make contact and would rather avoid interactions. The experience of switching is stressful, and customers feel that even if they switch, the new company may be just as bad as the one they left. Customers and providers end up with an uneasy relationship characterised by a reluctant inertia on the part of the customers to switch and providers focused on reducing servicing costs whilst ramping up prices for the customers. This flares up when customers have a frustrating time talking to call centres or chat lines and call-centre staff find themselves unable to help customers due to the constraints and rules they are bound by.

Another characteristic of the extractive approach is the use of marketing programmes where the focus is on up-selling, capturing customers, maximising the profit from each customer. The marketer is like the cowboy with the lasso. These marketing programmes will tend to involve aggressive selling, special offers only available to new customers, complex 'loyalty' programmes to buy customer loyalty, pricing designed to confuse customers into spending more than they need such as buy two get one free or bundled tariffs for energy, phone and broadband (Figure 1.2).

Attractive Thinking is different. It is about adding value for customers and seeking to attract more customers with better products rather than extracting value from the customers we already have. The attractive approach does not start with how to sell what we have already got and how to capture or trap customers into buying more stuff. Instead it seeks to understand the customer and find out what needs or problems they have. Then we work out how

Figure 1.2 Source: Marketoonist.com

the business can produce and deliver a solution to that need or problem. This 'attractive approach' or 'value adder approach' is[18] conjured up by this image of the person who is placing the final piece of the jigsaw. They have focused on identifying the shape of the hole in the jigsaw and then built the piece that makes the jigsaw complete. As a result, they are now ready to offer this perfectly shaped piece to the customer, so the customer's puzzle is now complete (Figure 1.3).

The attractive approach to business focuses on designing and building better products that help people solve problems in their day-to-day lives or day-to-day business. Remember that definition of marketing outlined by the Marketing Society 'to create sustainable growth by

---

[18] www.marketingsociety.com/the-library/only-consumers-can-make-capitalism-work/

Figure 1.3 Source: Ayzek (GoGraph)

understanding, anticipating and satisfying customer need'. This is the 'attractive approach' and is in contrast to the 'extractive approach' that focuses on how to get the most money from customers. The idea is that our business exists to make something that will solve a problem or address a physical or emotional need for people. This will mean that marketing and selling this 'something' will be easier. The marketing and selling job is now just to let people know about it and make it easy to buy. The marketing programmes associated with the 'value adder' and the attractive approach are: Advertising and social media to build awareness; incentives to try to experience the product; free sample products; partnerships to reach new audiences; distribution drives to create greater availability; digital that is easy to use and makes your 'something' easier to buy.

Mars have become and remain one of the world's largest privately owned food companies by building and designing brands and products that address specific human needs. All their brands were designed by starting with a need or problem that consumers have and then building products which offer outstanding quality and value for money to address that need. Mars Bar provides an energy boost, Snickers satisfies hunger, Twix accompanies a break, Dolmio makes your favourite Italian food easier to prepare, Maltesers are a chocolate hit without the calories and guilt, Pedigree makes feeding your pets easier. All these brands have had to adapt and modernise over the years as they run up against issues with changing consumer trends and priorities around healthy eating, attitudes to convenience, and intensified competition from other brands and from high-street innovation in cafes, sandwich bars, veterinary practices and home-cooking preferences. However, Mars continually adapt recipes, formats and availability to make sure the product remains a better product and is easy to buy. They make products that address real needs and problems, then the core of their marketing is brand building for awareness and reputation, and distribution and merchandising drives in the retail stores to make the product more visible and easier to buy.

In general, the consumer product giants, Unilever, P&G and Reckitt Benckiser take this kind of approach to building their brands. They seek to offer the best product in the market to satisfy consumer needs, they then can build a brand that has a reputation for doing that. Ariel washing powders and liquids, Cillit Bang cleaners and Dove soaps all deliver products that perform and offer value for money. These branded manufacturers know it is quite easy for their consumers to switch to another product. They also know if the product is not available in one store, their consumers will buy a competitor brand rather than go to another shop to find their preferred brand. They know that product must be easily available and easy to buy. They know they must delight the customer with every purchase and every time they use the product. They know that people can easily forget (lose awareness) of their brand, so awareness and recall is important. Unlike switching a bank account or broadband contract, switching your chocolate bar or soap powder choice is easy and painless and carries little risk. Trying a new product is also easy, painless and has negligible risk. They cannot trap their consumers; they must satisfy and delight them.

Interestingly these businesses have also seen the marketing science evidence (see Chapter 2) that shows that the size of their business and the amount of profit they make directly correlates with the number of customers and consumers that they have on any given day. They understand that market penetration is the biggest driver of profit. They are focused on attracting more customers to build their brands. Other sectors and businesses where this 'value adder' or 'attracting more customers' approach is prevalent exist in the high street such as coffee bars. Coffee bars are always trying to make their stores and products better. Costa talks about using better coffee beans; Caffè Nero celebrates their baristas; Starbucks focuses on welcoming ambience. Many restaurants, supermarkets and fashion stores take a similar approach, looking to make their offer more attractive, more suited to customer needs and always offering good value for money. These businesses relentlessly pursue better products and service as differentiators to attract more customers. They know they are solving day-to-day problems for everyday people and if their customers spot something better or have too many bad experiences they will try something else.

Industries dominated by value extractors are open to disruption. Several industries that were not delivering value, service and quality have been disrupted. Think about short-haul air travel before the arrival of low-cost carriers. Low-cost airlines such as EasyJet and Ryanair blew open the traditional high-cost approach taken by British Airways, Air France and many national carriers. They did not just attack price and value with low fares, they also focused on making their offer better. Tickets became easier to buy and to exchange. Tickets did not carry a series of complex provisions about return trip dates. We bought a simple ticket for one journey and that was that. The legacy carriers had created a complex system to protect the high charges they levied on frequent business passengers whilst offering some lower fares to leisure passengers. The low-cost carriers removed those barriers completely. However, now Ryanair and EasyJet are the established players, we have seen them adopt some value-extractive approaches in their pricing and marketing.

Unfortunately, train tickets are still like airline tickets used to be and remain complex with conditions that are easy for customers to breach and find themselves stranded. However, trains often have an effective monopoly on a route. Where a business can get monopoly control on a sector then the extractive approach looks irresistible. You can force customers to pay higher prices for a worse offer of product or service.

What is it that causes a business leader to choose between a value-adding approach and a value-extracting approach? There are three factors that will influence you:

1 the type of market and customer engagement with the product or service;

2 the existence of monopoly control over customers;

3 long vs short term and the commitment of management to building a sustainable long-term business.

Type of market

There are three market conditions that make the value extractive approach very risky and where more businesses will favour the 'attractive approach':

1 a market where consumers or customers find it easy to switch brands, no stress, no bother (think how easily you can switch your choice of chocolate bar vs how easy it is to switch bank accounts);

2 a market where people care about what they buy and what they choose (think of how you feel about which clothes you wear, or which drinks you consume vs how much you care which energy supplier you have);

3 a market where people enjoy the process of considering their choices e.g. buying clothes, choosing a coffee bar, restaurant or holiday.

Even though short-term gains can be had by saving costs, reducing quality, creating barriers to brand switching (loyalty programmes), in markets where the consumer is free to choose and it is easy to switch brands, the value-extractive approach is risky since the customers can easily 'find us out'. The attractive approach is more obviously needed in markets where customers care about having the best product for their mood and needs and find it easy to switch (e.g. chocolate bars) whereas the extractive approach tends to arise when it is hard for customers to switch and also they don't really care which brand or product they use and tend to feel that everyone is just as bad or as good as each other (e.g. bank accounts).

The converse is also true: That in markets where it is difficult or hard work for the customer to switch then the value extractive approach will seem more appealing. Customers generally do not enjoy spending time switching a bank account, shopping around for insurance, finding a new phone contract or switching their energy supplier. Most of us would rather be out enjoying ourselves, reading a book, meeting friends, watching TV, playing sport or whatever we really enjoy. If we know our customers are reluctant to switch, then it is tempting to find ways to make more profit from them as many will stick with you rather than endure the pain of a switch.

Another customer belief that encourages businesses to adopt the extractive approach is where people tend to believe that all providers are the same and just as good or bad as each other. If they switch, they are just jumping out of the frying pan into the fire. If the bank treats us badly, are we sure the next bank will be better?

Monopoly control over the market

The eighteenth-century economist Adam Smith was one of the first to note the conflict between the benefits of the free market that ensures economic prosperity for many and the desire of the business leader and property owner to exert control on the market so that they will not only obtain a price for their goods and services but can also 'extract a rent'. By 'rent' he means the ability to charge for non-productive activity: 'It is not from the benevolence of the butcher, the brewer, or the baker that we expect our dinner, but from their regard to their own interest.' Adam Smith explained that in a perfect free market the self-interest of the business person will be harnessed to provide what customers need. Free competition will drive businesses to deliver what customers want. The one that does it best at a fair price will be more successful and this creates prosperity for the whole economy. This drives a productive economy that makes things and services that add value for customers and expands the wider economy. This is what underpins 'Attractive Thinking'.

However, Smith also identified that businesses will seek to find ways to 'extract rent' (i.e. charge more) from the population. The ability to 'extract rent' can come from various sources:

- Owning property – rent apartments, houses, commercial property.

- Securing patents – blocking competitors out permits higher prices.

- Legal monopoly – e.g. a rail line can charge extra for high-demand periods.

- A famous brand – enables manufacturers to extract higher prices.

These are tools used in 'Extractive Thinking'. Rent in Smith's view does not add value, it extracts value. It is not inherently bad, but it does not add to the total productive economy. My point here is that if our business can extract rent in some form, it encourages us to take an extractive approach to customers. We will see later that whilst the extractive approach looks easier and will produce short-term gains, it is not the best way to create long-term value and a sustainable business.

Long term vs short term

Short-term value extracting is an easier and cheaper way to raise short-term profits. Management are clearly tempted to extract as much value as possible. We have seen this in the food industry. Here are a couple of examples.

Food and consumer product companies can get carried away and use an extractive approach. In November 2016 Mondelēz decided it would reduce the amount of chocolate in each Toblerone bar rather than put the price up to reflect increased costs. They also ensured the bar looked the same size on the shelf when in its box. This required them to create larger gaps between each chocolate peak in the bar. This was to maintain the size impression and the price point whilst delivering less. There were so many complaints about this that in July 2018 they reversed this decision. In trying to extract from/deceive/confuse customers they were losing customers even if they made a bit more profit on every bar.

The Mondelēz/Toblerone example is an extreme example of an approach adopted by many food companies to 'value engineer' their products to make more profit in the short term. They were caught out because it was so obvious. Other food brands have not been explicitly 'caught out' but end up offering worse value and a product that is not as good therefore consumers become less attached to the brand and product and over time the brand either grows less quickly or goes into decline.

Early in my marketing career, I was involved in a case study where we did the opposite and added quality back into a famous brand. I worked in the McVitie's marketing department and we were concerned about the amount of chocolate on the biscuits. We were worried the quality was not good enough. We had an idea the quality of the product was not as good as it used to be (this was hard to prove). This was a big concern when we were experiencing price competition from retail own-label products that were remarkably similar. We were asked by Eric Nicoli, the Managing Director of McVitie's, to create a business case to increase the chocolate on each biscuit.

After considerable consumer research and financial modelling, we presented a case for adding £1m back into the annual costs of the product and showed the sales increases we would need to create more profit. We also argued that continuing to lose market share to private label was not a viable position. It was not an easy argument to win. It is much easier to present an argument on how we might save money by financially engineering the product. In that case the saving would be guaranteed, the risk of losing sales seemed slight. But the reverse argument of let's add £1m to the cost and we might get more sales and we might get higher prices in the future was a harder one to trust. But it was the right decision and we won the day (in the end). Critically this argument would not have been won without the Managing Director championing the idea and the wider support from the board of directors.

Attracting vs extracting

We must recognise how we make decisions like this about what we produce, deliver and sell, how we price it, how we manage quality, how much this is led by customer need and how much this is led by short-term profit. Following this discussion of Attractive vs Extractive Thinking, we will know which of these approaches we favour instinctively. We will also have a sense of the balance of our decisions: are they mostly 'attractive' and 'adding value' or are they mostly 'extractive'?

All businesses operate with a mix of these attractive and extractive elements. The first question is how we maintain the balance, the second question is what is driving the agenda in our business and the third question is how we prioritise between the 14 critical numbers (that I listed earlier in the chapter) when making business decisions.

Attractive Thinking will show us how to make these decisions so that we attract more customers, create more value for our customers and build a profitable and sustainable business in both the short and the long term.

Game changers or market disruptors are usually value adders

Businesses and brands that disrupt industries usually create considerable growth opportunities both for them and other insurgent incomers. Disruption is not the only growth strategy, but when a business gets it right it is often spectacular. If they get it wrong, it is usually spectacularly expensive.

But what binds together all disruptors is that they always add value for customers. They always start with the customer. They deploy Attractive Thinking to attract customers away from established players to a new way to get a service or product. Very often they attract new customers into a market by making the product or service easier to buy, more affordable or more enjoyable to use. What is true is that they never start by using Extractive Thinking. Some switch to it later in their development but no-one ever disrupted an industry or market by seeking to extract more money from their existing customers. What is also true is the disruptors successfully grow their market:

- Monzo, Tide, Revolut are providing banking that is easier and more convenient to use and cheaper to run by harnessing mobile technology.

- OFX, TransferWise, Travelex and others took most of the foreign-exchange business away from traditional retail banks.

- First Direct established banking without branches and extraordinary customer service.

- Amazon: (need I say any more?).

- Virgin Atlantic brought value and service to trans-atlantic airline travel.

- Celebrations chocolates reinvigorated the casual chocolate gift market when Roses and Quality Street were taking it for granted (my own small contribution to this list).

- Pharmaceutical switches: Every time a medicine is switched from being restricted to prescription only to being sold over the counter then the product ends up being easier to buy, more people can be treated and often it is cheaper, so real value is added e.g. Nurofen, Ella One, Zantac, Voltarol, Imodium.

In mobile phones there were three disruptions. The car phone, the mobile phone – which started large and heavy and got smaller – then the iPhone, which killed Nokia. Apple chose a careful balance of value extraction (locked systems and high prices) and value adding (stunning design and ease of use) to attract customers and grow their business. I would argue that the value add created by Apple through superior design and functionality was so huge that they were able to extract additional rent through high prices and locked systems without much harm. They built a monopoly control over their users. But as Samsung and Huawei have chased them with similar design, lower cost models and better distribution, the dynamic of the market is changing, and I would argue that only an Attractive Thinking approach will work in the future. Apple is now pursuing privacy control as a point of difference.

Another category of disruptive business that create massive added value for consumers are the new tech platform intermediaries that facilitate transactions between providers and customers: Airbnb, HomeAway, Expedia, Booking.com, Uber, Deliveroo. They have grown customer demand for products and they have sometimes brought down prices (Uber taxis vs black cab, Airbnb vs hotels). They have created opportunities for providers to earn extra money or even make a living (room renting on Airbnb, Uber taxi drivers).

But as these businesses start to exert control on the markets, they are no longer disruptors, they are the market. Then the temptation to become value extractors arises and these platforms are extracting too much value. The platform charges either the customer or the provider a fee or commission. The question is: Does the fee provide enough value to the customer and the provider? If they get this balance right, they will continue to prosper and be true disruptors and value adders. When they get this wrong, it is likely the markets will slow down as providers refuse to deliver stock to the platform and customers resist the charges.

Attractive Thinking is the best approach. This is not a moral or principled position that this is somehow superior but is a practical belief that it just works better. In the next chapters we will examine some rules and evidence about customers and markets and how they work to demonstrate why Attractive Thinking is the best way. Then we will look at how we can offer value in PINPOINT, POSITION, PERFECT, PROMOTE and PITCH.

Four insights from customers are pivotal

If we are to start with the customer, it is helpful to focus on the different steps that the customer will go through when they buy our products and services.

There are four steps in the customer experience (Figure 1.4). Some marketers call this the customer journey. What matters for us is how well we perform at each step. We must succeed at all of them to make a sale and create an advocate who will recommend our product and service to others.

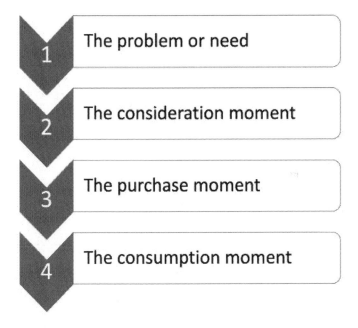

Figure 1.4 Four moments in the customer experience

Once we understand how well we perform at each step, we can decide what is the priority area to attract more customers. Either we need to develop stronger 'pull' strategies (e.g. brand building and advertising), adopt a 'push' approach (e.g. improve distribution and availability), improve our likability (improve design or customer experience) or increase our visibility (more promotion or on shelf or web standout).

The problem or need

A fundamental truth of business (and life) is that no-one ever put their hand in their pocket to spend money unless they experience a problem or need. People don't buy your stuff to be nice to the brand; they don't buy it just because they like us (they probably won't buy if they don't like us). They hand over their money or their credit card because they have an issue or need or want to get something done and they have decided we can help them. These problems and needs fall into various categories. Here are a few:

- physical e.g. hunger, tired, cold, hot, lose weight, get fitter;

- emotional e.g. bored, seeking to impress, wanting to be social, lonely;

- financial e.g. security, managing money, saving, creating income;

- success e.g. business, social, personal goals, happiness;

- family and friends e.g. express love, stay close, communicate;

- safety e.g. manage risk, avoid danger, protection.

The United Nations has produced another list based on its global goals for sustainable development (Figure 1.5). This list also indicates for us several human needs and problems that different businesses could address. These are things that occupy our minds, and everyone is preoccupied with at least some of these. Look to see if your business can act to work in one of these areas.

Figure 1.5 United Nations Sustainable Development Goals. *Source:*
United Nations, www.un.org/sustainabledevelopment/
sustainable-development-goals/

The customer starts with a problem and not a brand

Too often, I see business owners, managers and marketers
assume that people are thinking about their brands and
choosing between brands depending on whether they
like the brands and what features and benefits they offer.
But the customer does not start with our product, they
start with a problem. The problem will be related to
something on one of these lists.

Think about when we go to the supermarket. The initial
visit is not inspired by a love of Waitrose or Aldi or Tesco
but is driven by our need to stock up some cupboards, to
entertain guests, to feed the family or simply a desire to go
out and do something, get out of the house, a change of
scene. Then once there at the shop (online or in-store),
we are thinking about a list of occasions and needs and
choosing the products that best fulfil those. What is on our

mind is replacing some essentials like cleaning materials, condiments, tea, coffee, etc. Then there might be some occasions or events that I need stuff for, family meal times, going out on picnic, people coming round, a special party. It is these occasions and needs that are driving decisions about what types of things to buy.

In Attractive Thinking we need to start by understanding what the problem is that our product solves or what the need is that it addresses and how well we do it. We explore this in PINPOINT.

Note on business purpose and customer problem

The problem we are solving also guides the purpose of our business. Having a business purpose works when it is the purpose of our business. So, I am arguing that the best way to define our business purpose is to look at the way we solve our customers' problems and what we do around that. When Mitesh Sheth of Redington (pensions investment consultants) says they exist to help 100 million people become financially secure, the purpose makes sense because the problem they are solving is to plug pension deficits in company pension schemes. The two are connected. When our business purpose is not what we actually do, it is seen as fake and customers see through it. So, when Gillette says their purpose is help men be 'The Best Men Can Be' and to respect women, the connection with razors is weak. When Heineken exhorts us all to be more open to other people's ideas, this is only slightly connected to the activity of having a beer.

The consideration moment

At this point the customer has become aware of a need and is starting to consider how they might address it. They are considering options and weighing them up.

This could be a process that takes a millisecond (picking up salt in the supermarket) or several weeks/months (planning a holiday or buying a car) or a short while (choosing clothing or a gift). It might involve substantial research (choosing a mortgage).

By far the most important thing here is to be in the customer's mind and have created awareness both in the past and at the moment of consideration. People buy things that they are familiar with and like. Being familiar means getting to know something or someone over a period of time. This creates trust. Likability comes from personal experience or the experience of friends and family.

Awareness, trust and likability are the key factors at this point. How people react to brands and product choices has some similarity with how people react to others and their choice to form a relationship with them or not. The first time we meet a person we are a bit reserved and wary of them, then the more times we meet we start to build trust. The more experience we have then we start to like them more (or not). It is the same for people and for brands.

What this means for us whether selling soap or high-end business services is that we need to find ways of creating awareness first. Awareness growth is a leading indicator of future business growth and declining awareness suggests declining sales in the future. The first time people see us or hear of us is not often the time they buy. We need to build our way into their consideration moments over time. See POSITION on developing likability and PROMOTE on creating awareness.

The purchase moment

This follows the consideration moment. The moment of picking up the credit card and entering it online or handing it over in a shop. The most significant factor here is simply being available and visible. I have long argued that the reasons Coca-Cola is the biggest soft-drink brand in the world are first that is available in more places than any other drink; second that it is more visible both in store, on the street and in the media; and third that it created a likeable product and brand. The most important things are that it is in the consumer's mind and is extremely easy to buy.

The reason Amazon is heading to be the biggest retailer in the world is that it is the easiest to use and the easiest to buy from. The products are available, the checkout is fast and easy, delivery and returns are straightforward. It is in this territory of the purchase moment that Amazon dominates.

What this means for us are things such as the search ranking on Google, the prominence of display in-store, the position on the shelf, the ease of finding on a website, the smoothness of the checkout experience, the reminder advertising at the moment of purchase so products don't get forgotten.

We will see in Chapter 2 just how important awareness and visibility are. This is based on the rules of how customers and prospects behave and how markets actually work.

The consumption moment

This is after the customer bought our product or service and the experience they have consuming or using it. In the case of food, this is usually about taste, texture, how satisfying it is and what other people think about it, there is a social dimension. In the case of web apps or online shopping, does it do what I expect, is it easy to use, is it no bother, is it absorbing? In the case of business services, it is usually about whether the business improvement actually took place and whether the events and work delivered what was promised. Did using this service make my business more successful?

Having success at this point is obviously important to ensure the customer buys again. It also determines whether the customer becomes an advocate and helps us recruit more customers via the most often used and most powerful marketing tool in the whole marketing armoury: *Word of mouth.*

Summary

We have explored five things we should have in our business to keep our focus on the customer.

First, create a customer mindset and not a supplier mindset. Relentlessly look at what matters to customers and keep focused on what makes their experience better rather than what is clever, difficult or challenging for us to deliver.

Second, monitor the four success factors that drive a high-growth business. Make sure someone is responsible for the value proposition:

1 A value proposition for our customers that is relevant, distinctive and differentiated.

2 They communicate it with sufficient power.

3 They make sure they deliver it every time and every day.

4 The business has basic economics that work.

We explore how to create a value proposition and communicate it with sufficient power in Part II.

Third, consider whether we drive profit by adding value to attract more customers or extracting more profit from existing customers. Do we have the right balance?

Make it explicit in our business. If we want to really step up our growth or disrupt a market or be a game changer in our industry, then we need to invest in adding value to our customers. It is the only way.

Fourth, ensure we understand the four stages of our customer journey and use our understanding of these four steps to keep our team in a customer mindset at all times:

1   the problem or need;

2   the consideration moment;

3   the purchase moment;

4   the consumption moment.

Fifth, remember our business purpose is to solve a customer problem and address a need. The business purpose is our core activity, not a nice to do 'add on'.

If we must start with the customer to guide our business decisions, then how do we understand our customers? This is the subject of the next chapter.

Chapter 2

How to understand customers

Where does market research fit in to understanding customers?

In the previous chapter, I did not mention market research as a tool to help us think like a customer and to make sure we start with what the customer wants. That was deliberate. I do believe market research has a role to play, but it is a limited role and one that must be used carefully. Understanding customers and customer mindset is a carefully curated mixture of art and science. Market research is one component of that mixture. It can be amazingly revealing; it can also be extremely dangerous. The most important thing is that it must be used in the context of all the other insight, data, information and experience that we have at our disposal.

In this chapter we will explore quite a few different approaches to understanding customers. We will explore some data, some opinion based on experience, some strong evidence-based marketing science and the role of market research. Later when we look at PINPOINT, POSITION, PERFECT and PROMOTE, I will refer to different market research tools that we can use to add to our insight and customer knowledge. But we only use market research when there is a business decision to take; there are other data we can check and there are valid questions that we can ask customers to which we can reasonably get valid answers. We will look at research techniques we can conduct ourselves and ones we may get professionals to do for us.

What can we ask customers?

There are a blistering array of market research tools and techniques. Professional market researchers offer usage and attitude studies, omnibus studies, retail audit, consumer panel data on behaviours and attitudes, brand tracking, concept testing, packaging testing, pricing testing, market simulation, ethnographic research, focus groups and modelling and the list goes on. In addition to professional market research, there are self-help online tools such as Survey Monkey, Survey Gizmo and Smart Surveys; these help anyone to set up a survey and find things out from their customers and get customer feedback. Social media enthusiasts will also show us ways we can get customer insight and customer feedback from smart reading of and listening to our social media channels.

The trick to finding the right approach is to start with the question 'what do I want to find out and what decision do I want to take?' Now amidst all these techniques there are only three underlying questions that we ever try to answer. They are:

1   What should I be doing?

2   How well am I doing it?

3   How will the customer respond when I do it?

Market research involves asking customers questions and getting their reactions or observing and measuring customer behaviour. Market research is particularly useful, but it can only really help with the first two. And market research should not be taken too literally; it should only provide a partial support to our own intuition and experience.

The underlying insight here is that customers are good at telling us about their previous experiences; they have valuable insight into their needs and desires, but have a very poor ability to anticipate what they might do in the future, what we might create in the future and how they might react to that. We will look at each of these three types of question.

What should I be doing?

This question can be broken down into specific questions such as: What new product should we launch? What need or problem do customers have that we could address? How can we improve the product or service to make it more attractive? This question is about how to optimise our value proposition and about how we communicate our value proposition to let people know about it and make it available so they can buy it.

Experience shows it is unwise to ask customers directly, what should we be doing? A direct question to get their ideas on what we should do is not likely to be that inspiring or helpful. If we do that, the customer has no idea what we are capable of and I would suggest we are better than them at that and it is our job to create ideas about what we could do.

But there is something much more valuable that we can do to inform our ideas about what we should do. We can ask them about their experiences, so ask about their needs, frustrations and problems. This is valuable. We exist to 'create a customer' and solve a problem for that customer. A customer is looking for things that help them solve a problem.

We can also ask them what is important to them and what does not matter. In other words, we can get insight into their experiences and problems. Somewhere in that work we will get an insight into what we can do to help them.

Examples of professionally provided services that do this are usage and attitude studies, consumer panel data, omnibus studies, brand tracking, qualitative focus groups and ethnographic research. We can use these and other tools I will discuss in POSITION. Once we know what it is that we should be doing to attract more customers then we move on to assess the next question.

How well am I doing it?

The most common form of this is the customer satisfaction study or customer feedback survey. A popular and frequently quoted measure of this type of question is the Net Promoter Score (NPS) ®. NPS measures the number of people advocating or recommending our product or service and the number of people not recommending or detracting from our product or service. The difference between these two measures is our NPS. A positive score is good, and a negative score is bad. The consultancy firm Bain & Company has analysis to suggest that this score is a real indicator of the ability of a business to create long-term value. Value adders will get a great NPS:[19]

---

[19] www.bain.com/insights/introducing-the-net-promoter-system-loyalty-insights/

Asking the ultimate question allows companies to track promoters and detractors, producing a clear measure of an organisation's performance through its customers' eyes, its Net Promoter Score®. Bain analysis shows that sustained value creators—companies that achieve long-term profitable growth—have Net Promoter Scores (NPS) two times higher than the average company. And Net Promoter System® leaders on average grow at more than twice the rate of competitors.

We should always measure how well we are doing. As creators and marketers, we are unable to assess this as well as our customers can. The question 'How well am I doing it?' is one that market research is well equipped to help us answer. But then we come to the third question. This is a question that customers are poorly equipped to answer in market research.

How will the customer respond when I do it?

This is the million-dollar question that every CEO, marketer and business owner wants to know the answer to. We all want to know: Will the customer buy it? Will they respond to our ad? Will they respond to our product or message? We will spend a lot of money bringing a product or a marketing campaign to market. Quite reasonably, we want to know 'will it work?'. And in response to this demand for a reassuring answer the market research business has produced a plethora of tools to answer it. But there is a fundamental problem here. The problem is that forecasting is fraught with issues. And this question is asking for a prediction.

As people we are unable to predict exactly what we will do tomorrow, let alone what we will buy or how we will react to an advertising campaign. We do not know how we will feel about the choices we will face. Our customers and prospects are just like us. Even if they think they will buy the product in the future, they cannot be sure. This problem is further compounded by the test environment. In a market research exercise prospects are removed from the context in which they would make a decision. They are unable to make a reliable prediction.

As a result of understanding this issue tools have been created to simulate market conditions and observe behaviour rather than asking questions. A leading example is the BASES test from Nielsen.[20] These tools simulate the market either in a test environment or a real shopping environment. But these have also hit problems. When the predictions are shown to be wrong, the test provider will demonstrate that the real product or market turned out differently from the simulation. If the product or market had been like the simulation, then their forecast would have come true. Whilst this argument defends the integrity of the test methodology, it does not help the creator and marketer of the product. We did not predict the market environment that we will face. So, the test prediction was not correct.

The market research business has worked hard at developing these tools, because CEOs wish to mitigate future risk and get reassurances that the investments, product launches and marketing campaigns will work. But these tools provide an illusion of reassurance. That is all it is.

The only way to find out how the customer will respond is to put the product in a real market with real customers. This is what is behind the idea of minimal

---

[20] www.nielsen.com/uk/en/solutions/product-development.html

viable product as advocated by Eric Ries in *The Lean Startup*.[21] He learned the hard way that it is a mistake to invest heavily in a perfect product before we know it will work. He only started to succeed when he made the absolute minimum product and exposed it to customers to get a reaction. This was not using market research, but by seeing if they bought it and then finding out how they reacted after they used it. This is much easier in the world of digital product and is common practice. In the world of physical product, it is harder to make an imperfect product and take it to market. Sometimes we are forced to get a reaction to a prototype or concept board and work from there (see PERFECT). But be wary of results from artificial situations.

The inability to predict how customers will react has also led to the popularity of digital direct response advertising. This is another form of real testing in real conditions. Quite simply this medium makes it easy to create a message or a test product or test sale of a product online and then track precise customer response. This measurability and predictability overcomes the problems of trying to test in synthetic environments. We are testing for real. This is immensely attractive.

In POSITION, we will see that if we reliably find out what matters to customers and then design our product or campaign to deliver that, our chances of success are much increased and give better odds than relying on market research concept tests.

To reiterate, we must not take notice of the answers to the survey question 'Will you buy this?'. The customer is unable to give us a reliable answer. Instead we should put our effort into understanding the answer to the first

---

[21] Eric Ries (2011) *The Lean Startup*, Crown Publishing.

two questions. Market research and other tools can help us with these questions:

1   What should I be doing?

2   How well am I doing it?

For the third question: 'How will the customer respond when I do it?' i.e. 'Will the customer buy it?', we should be considering how to develop a minimum viable product so that we can test a real product with real customers to see if they will buy it and what they will use it for.

Customer behaviour follows some rules

A large amount of marketing and brand advice is based on people's theories of how things work. A lot of the advice makes sense, so it is easy to adopt and follow. Some of the advice only comes from theories rather than evidence and can lead us down the wrong path. However, we can counter this. There is an increasingly large body of marketing science that is looking for evidence to guide us. Here are some rules that come from that work. These rules can guide what we do.

> *Rule 1:* Many more customers buy bigger brands than buy smaller brands and those customers buy bigger brands only slightly more often than they buy smaller brands.

Bigger businesses have more customers than smaller businesses. This is always true within any given market. Another way of making this point is 'no business ever got growth without getting more customers'. When businesses decline it is because they are losing customers. It is not because the same number of customers is buying less. Now this is not logically and necessarily the case. We could observe two training businesses as described in the example below:

	Number of customers	Purchases per year	Price	Revenue	Market share
Business 1	1,000	2	10	20,000	10%
Business 2	100	20	10	20,000	10%

One business sells training programmes to 1,000 customers who each buy 2 programmes a year. The other business sells training programmes to 100 customers who on average buy 20 programmes a year each. In this example both businesses would have the same revenue and the same market share of the segment. In theory this is possible. In practice it never happens like this. In practice it always looks like this:

	Number of customers	Purchases per year	Price	Revenue	Market share
Business 1	1,000	3	10	30,000	15%
Business 2	100	2	10	2,000	1%

The business with more customers would be much bigger because it has many more customers who would buy slightly more often than the customers of the smaller business.

The first person to discover this and publish about this was a professor at London Business School and later South Bank University called Andrew Ehrenberg.[22] He wrote about this in numerous academic papers and presented about this

---

[22] A. Ehrenberg (1966) Laws in marketing – A tailpiece, *Journal of the Royal Statistical Society*, Series C, 15, 257–268. A. Ehrenberg

at conferences. His findings were based on many case studies. He built up an empirical evidence base that showed that in every market he examined there was a correlation between the penetration of the market by a brand or company and its market share. (Our market penetration is the percentage of all the possible customers in that market that buy our product. Our market share is our revenue from sales in that market expressed as a percentage of the revenues from all products in that market.)

The thing that most astonished Andrew Ehrenberg was the reaction to this work. Marketers and ad agencies argued that he was wrong because it did not fit their theoretical model of customers and behaviour that they believed. He challenged the idea that creating customer loyalty is the key to growth. I first came across Ehrenberg's work in the 1980s and was struck by its clarity and the evidence base behind it. I was equally flabbergasted at marketers' reaction to it and the tendency to favour pet theories and anecdotes over a systematic and more scientific approach to collecting evidence (Figure 2.1).

Ehrenberg did not give up. He attracted an academic and practitioner team, including Australian marketing academic Byron Sharp to conduct further research into the science of customer behaviour, the ways that marketing works and how customers actually respond in practice. They formed the Ehrenberg Bass Institute based out of the University of South Australia in Adelaide and South Bank University in London. The purpose of the team is to create an evidence-based understanding of customer behaviour

---

(1968) The elements of lawlike relationships, *Journal of the Royal Statistical Society*, Series A, 131, 280–329. A. Ehrenberg (1969) The discovery and use of laws of marketing, *Journal of Advertising Research*, 9, 2, 11–17.

Figure 2.1 Source: Marketoonist.com

and brand performance and use this to help companies influence their marketing, advertising and product development. For many years this work was only available on a private basis to the corporate sponsors who paid for this research work. This included many leading global brands such as Nestlé, ESPN, Google, P&G and Unilever. This undoubtedly created an advantage for these brand giants as they learned how to maintain their leadership.

In 2010 Byron Sharp published a book for everyone called *How Brands Grow* that explained the main findings of their research. In this book Sharp asserts that it is time for marketing to grow up and become more scientific in its understanding of customers.[23] In his TEDx talk he argues

---

[23] Byron Sharp (2010) *How Brands Grow: What Marketers Don't Know,* Oxford University Press. Jenni Romanuik and Byron Sharp (2015) *How Brands Grow: Part 2: Emerging Markets, Services, Durables, New and Luxury Brands,* Oxford University Press.

that medicine was transformed by evidence and science throughout the twentieth century and this continues today. But before science intervened in medicine doctors used theories of treatment (leeches, bloodletting) that may well have killed more people than they saved. Since medicine moved to an evidence-based scientific approach it has been more successful in treating people and saving lives.[24]

Much of marketing still seems stuck in theories about how things work rather than examining evidence of what actually happens. As a result, some marketing stuff we read about is little more than a theory. Sharp floated a series of what he called 'laws of marketing'. The first and I believe most significant of these is what I have called Rule 1.

> *Rule 1:* Many more customers buy bigger brands than buy smaller brands and those customers buy bigger brands only slightly more often than they buy smaller brands.

The point is that to grow a brand we must attract more customers and increase our penetration of the market. The difference between smaller and bigger brands is not how many times people buy our product or how much they buy on each occasion; the difference is explained by how many customers we have. In marketing jargon: Penetration is king. To grow our brand we must find more customers.

> *Rule 2:* Customer loyalty is a mirage, customers are not 'loyal' in an emotional sense. They

---

[24] Byron Sharp, The science of marketing, TEDx Adelaide 2010, https://youtu.be/d3Or0FkiIa0

have habits. They buy our brand for as long as it suits them, when they stop buying it is either because they don't need it any more or they found an alternative that is more suited to their needs.

Figure 2.2 Source: Marketoonist.com

The most striking evidence for this comes from Ehrenberg Bass. The data show that defection rates from one brand in any market are pretty much the same for all the other brands in the same market. The reason for this is that the dominant reason for not buying a brand any more is not the failure of the brand or that some brands are better at conjuring up loyalty; the real reasons are not to do with the brand, they are to do with the customer. For example:

- Ski Club of Great Britain membership: *The member stopped going skiing.*

- Airline: *Customer stopped going to the place(s) where they used the service before.*

- Nappies: *Children grew up.*

- Regional banks: *Customer moved to a new area.*

- Food and drink: *My usual shop stopped selling it, it was not available.*

- Any: *A new cheaper and better alternative arrived on the market.*

- Business hotel: *Guest stopped visiting clients in that city.*

Because the main reasons for defecting are driven by customer needs and are a characteristic of the market, then the defection rates are common to all the brands. It is true that bigger brands have slightly more loyalty than smaller brands and get bought slightly more often. But what this means is that the number of customers defines which brand is biggest or smallest (see rule 1). Usually the reason the biggest brand is bought a bit more often than the smallest brand is that bigger brands have better awareness, are easier to recall, are easier to buy, have more availability in store, are more visible in Google.

Now this is not to say that customer loyalty does not matter. It matters that customers are enthusiastic about our brand or product. After all, they are the biggest advocates that encourage more customers to buy the brand. Existing customers are the key to getting more customers. They can easily act as a detractor to cause us to have fewer customers if they have a bad experience.

What this does say is we should not try to buy the loyalty of our customers with expensive discounts, loyalty programme and other costly incentives. The scientific evidence is that we cannot make much impact on their loyalty with these tools. We must earn our loyalty not try to bribe people to be loyal. What really drives loyalty is whether the customer still needs the brand, can they remember and recall our brand when they need it, is it available and easy to buy when they need it and whether they had a good experience last time or have a recommendation from friends and family that they trust. These are the loyalty drivers. Funnily enough they are also the drivers of how to attract new customers.

> *Rule 3:* Brand reputation is firstly what drives customers to buy and will determine our profitability and underpin our growth.

One of the most serious traps a business owner or marketer can be caught out by is the temptation to believe that if only we could sell it for a lower price, then we would sell more. This is fuelled by our personal experience as a consumer that we are tempted by things that cost less. We all like to save a bit of money. But there are two pieces of evidence that challenge the assumption that offering a discount or a lower price will drive more sales revenue.

The first evidence is that data across markets show us that the cheapest products or services on offer only represent around 10–20% of the total market. This means that the other 80–90% of sales is accounted for by customers choosing to pay more. I have personally seen this in chocolate, soft drinks, gardening products, ski holidays, training, business consultants, law firms, accountancy. This hard evidence points us to the observation that people are looking for something good rather than cheap. Yes, they want good value for money and if they see two offers that are identical on quality and relevance, then they will choose the less expensive one.

The second evidence is from a study that started in 2007 and was conducted by Les Binet and Peter Field on behalf of the Institute of Practitioners in Advertising (IPA). This shows that any increase in profitable sales due to marketing activity is usually explained by an improvement in brand reputation and awareness.

The first publication of this finding was in 2007 in a book called *Marketing in the Era of Accountability*. It was an analysis of 980 submissions to the IPA Marketing Effectiveness Awards. These submissions provide unique data about marketing campaigns and their commercial effectiveness. This work has continued, and updates have been published in further publications, *The Long and the Short of It* (2013), *Media in Focus: Marketing Effectiveness in the Digital Era* (2017) and *Effectiveness in Context* (2018).[25]

Binet and Field have repeatedly discovered that marketing campaigns that build brand reputation and strengthen a customer's emotional connection with the brand have a greater impact on sales, are more cost-effective and deliver more long-term profit than

---

[25] Les Binet and Peter Field (2007) *Marketing in the Era of Accountability*, IPA. Les Binet and Peter Field (2013) *The Long and the Short of It*, IPA. Les Binet and Peter Field (2017) *Media in Focus: Marketing Effectiveness in the Digital Era*, IPA. Les Binet and Peter Field (2018) *Effectiveness in Context*, IPA.

marketing campaigns that deliver discounts, short-term promotions, competitions or only activate short-term sales. There is an overwhelming correlation between building brand reputation, creating an emotional connection with a brand and increasing profitable sales.

Examples of campaign tools that build reputation and the emotional connections would be:

- TV advertising or YouTube ads (depends on the approach);
- partnerships with other brands or stars;
- word of mouth recommendations;
- Facebook ads (depends on the approach).

Examples of short-term activities that will activate short-term sales would be:

- direct mail;
- money-off promotion in-store;
- competition with prize;
- discount if you buy before a certain date;
- Google Ads.

This brings us to rule 4, which is about the role of these short-term sales promotional activities.

> *Rule 4:* Short-term sales activation effects are only short term.

A customer will experience our brand in different ways. Broadly these can be summed up as:

1   observing and seeing advertising and marketing messages e.g. TV, print or online ad;

2   a feeling that they like or dislike the brand or its brand personality e.g. brand emotion;

3   being propositioned or proposed by a sales offer or sales person e.g. in-store offer or direct mail;

4   being recommended by someone they trust e.g. family and friends;

5   actually using and experiencing the product or service;

6   being offered a follow-up to buy again e.g. broadband provider offers mobile phone contract or TV service.

Their view of our product or service will be conditioned by some combination of these. Whether or not they buy depends on whether they need or want our product to help them address a need or solve a problem (see PINPOINT). If the need exists, then each of these six influences kicks in to determine which product or service they buy. These six different experiences add up to the brand experience.

Unfortunately for us marketers the biggest influence on brand experience is from the two things that are hardest to control. Namely recommendations from a person they trust and their personal experience of using the product or service. This is down to the design and delivery of the product or service (see PERFECT).

But the marketer's armoury of advertising, direct marketing, sales promotion, loyalty programmes and follow-up offers do have an effect. To design our campaigns, we must split these activities into 'above the line' and 'below the line'. This is the same distinction as brand building and sales activation.

Brand building (above the line) is about creating awareness, building familiarity and creating an emotional connection with the brand. It is the sense from the customer that they know what the brand offers, have heard about it before, know it is used by other people they trust, they like the company that makes it, it is all intuitive and emotional. This is just the same as getting to know a person. When we first meet a person, we are naturally wary and maybe even uncomfortable. As we get to know them more, we become more familiar, like them more and trust them and will choose to spend more time with them (or not if we don't like them).

Sales activation (below the line) is all about prompting the customer to buy or 'closing the sale'. This is a time-limited discount, a direct mail offer, a display and promotion in the shop or the e-commerce site. This is about visibility, noticeability and a reason to buy now.

We can learn about this by thinking of personal relationships: if we try to 'activate' a relationship before we get to know someone, then it is likely we will be rejected. If we meet someone and then within 30 seconds say: 'Let's meet for dinner' this makes them uncomfortable. Whereas if we build the relationship first in small tiny steps, such as let's meet for coffee, then we will more likely be accepted. Eventually there comes a point where activating the relationship feels right for both people. It is the same for brands, products and services.

The Binet and Field work in *Marketing in the Era of Accountability* produced two important findings for marketers.

The first finding is that the campaigns which deployed both brand building and sales activation in a balanced mix were far more successful than campaigns that focused on one or the other. The optimal mix is 60:40 in favour of brand activation. This finding has been tested repeatedly. It keeps coming back with the same answer. The most effective campaigns invest 60% of their activity in brand building and 40% in sales activation.

The second finding is that sales activation activity has a very marked and dramatic effect on short-term sales, but this only lasts for the duration of the activity. Once the activity stops then sales drop away again whereas brand building activity has a long-term effect. It is a much slower burn.

> *Rule 5:* Brand building investment is essential
> to create long-term brand value and profit.

Pound for pound and dollar for dollar, sales activation produces a much bigger short-term sales lift than brand building. However, brand building produces a long-term benefit that lasts beyond the campaign. This means that if we keep repeating a brand building investment it is possible to build the brand reputation step by step. But if we only do sales activation investment then we will experience short-term sales lifts but no long-term gain in the brand reputation.

Figure 2.3 illustrates the effects that were identified by Binet and Field in *Marketing in the Era of Accountability* (2007) and updated in *Media in Focus: Marketing Effectiveness in the Digital Era* (2017). We can see that initially the brand does not get a return on investment but after that the returns just get better and better. This shows the problem with convincing a

CEO or finance director that brand investment will pay out. It is easier to be tempted by the sales activation promise of quick returns than the promise of longer term benefits and financial returns that come next year or the year after. To build the brand we must spend money on marketing that will not pay back within 12 months. The work by Binet and Field demonstrates that it is in the shareholders' interest to make this investment. But this is a tough decision to make when we cannot see a quick return.

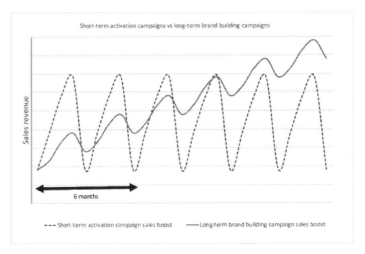

Figure 2.3 Theoretical illustration of the sales effects of short term campaigns vs long term brand building campaigns

The work by Ehrenberg, Sharp, Binet and Field has helped marketers understand how markets work and how customers behave in practice. There are more findings and insights than I have covered here in this chapter. But for me, the five rules of customer behaviour that I have picked out are the top five and the ones I will refer to as we discuss how to attract more customers in Chapters 5 to 9. In summary, these five rules are:

Rule 1: Many more customers buy bigger brands than buy smaller brands and they buy bigger brands slightly more often than they buy smaller brands.

Rule 2: Customer loyalty is a mirage, customers are not 'loyal' in an emotional sense. They have habits. They buy our brand for as long as it suits them, when they stop buying it is either because they don't need it any more or they found an alternative that is more suited to their needs.

Rule 3: Brand reputation is firstly what drives customers to buy and will determine our profitability and underpin our growth.

Rule 4: Short-term sales activation effects are only short term.

Rule 5: Brand building investment is essential to create long-term brand value and profit.

The picture of the customer that emerges from these rules is that strong brands are not dominated by a few passionate loyal customers, but rather by lots of customers who have busy lives and easily forget about a brand, product or service unless they are frequently reminded by frequent use or frequent marketing. These customers are not loyal, they are creatures of habit and easily influenced by their needs. If it is difficult to switch brands (e.g. bank accounts) they will not do it very often, if it is easy to switch brands (e.g. soft drinks) they will do it a lot and very easily. Our job is to add value and solve their problem.

This is just as true for high-end B2B professional services, luxury brands, financial services, utility brands, leisure and travel as it is for consumer products. Customers easily forget about our brand unless we keep reminding them. They have busy lives; they are preoccupied with other things.

One of the most valuable concepts is the idea of customers having a repertoire of brands and that repertoire is constantly evolving. This repertoire is nearly always three to six brands with some brands surviving for years while others just come and go. In snacks I might have a repertoire of Graze bars, Kettle Chips, fruit bowl, salad pot, Lindt dark chocolate and Twix. Then from time to time this might evolve to include Kit Kat and Eat Natural. Often this repertoire would simply be due to what was available in the shop or coffee bar or sandwich store. Or might be because I noticed something I had not had for some time and was reminded to try it.

This insight into the casual nature of customer decision making means brand awareness and top of mind awareness are essential. Simply being remembered and recalled can be enough to trigger repurchase of an old favourite.

Now I know you are thinking yes that is all fine for big brands and consumer brands but my market is different. This analysis has been tested across tech brands, financial services, durables such as cars and domestic equipment. The dynamics do vary between the markets, but the fundamental insights remain. See *How*

Brands Grow: Part 2,[26] *Marketing: Theory, Evidence, Practice*[27] and *Effectiveness in Context.*[28] People may only buy a car every three to six years, but they have a repertoire of consideration and they evolve their decision with many factors over a period of time. In the end the purchase is down to brand trust and emotion, product suitability and possibly sealed by some offers and negotiation at the time of purchase.

In financial services people would rather go to the dentist than spend time considering the various offers made by banks and insurance companies. Again repertoire, habit, awareness and recommendation are very influential.

This takes us to the next element of understanding the customer and this is about what to measure and how to do it.

Create measures and get them accepted

What gets measured gets managed.[29]

Having measurements, even if they are subjective ones, is a powerful way to engage our colleagues in things we all agreed we should do. It is the best way to get support from other people for our plans and actions in the business.

---

[26] Jenni Romanuik and Byron Sharp (2015) *How Brands Grow: Part 2: Emerging Markets, Services, Durables, New and Luxury Brands,* Oxford University Press.

[27] Byron Sharp (2012) *Marketing: Theory, Evidence, Practice,* Oxford University Press.

[28] Les Binet and Peter Field (2018) *Effectiveness in Context,* IPA.

[29] Peter Drucker (1954, 2007) *The Practice of Management,* Routledge.

This is a subject that preoccupies managers and consultants. The most well-known tool is The Balanced Score Card by Robert Kaplan and David Norton and published in the *Harvard Business Review* in 1992.[30] The idea is a business should track a wider range of measures than purely financial ones. This means the board will be able to take better decisions to promote the growth, profitability and general well-being of the business.

If we want to attract more customers to our business, then we need some measures of our progress. These measures should relate to the four pivotal insights about the customer journey. Here are some suggestions on what we can measure.

The problem or need

If we are creating a new brand, we need to know if the problem or need matters enough to customers so that people will spend money to solve it. Does it matter to enough customers so that we can create a viable business to address it?

For an existing brand we need to know whether the problem we solve matters to more and more people or whether fewer are becoming interested in this. Is it becoming supplanted by another problem that makes the original problem less relevant? We need to find ways to track this.

In food there are new trends all the time. Consumers are getting concerned about different issues and attracted to different tastes over time. Veganism is on the rise due to

---

[30] Robert Kaplan and David Norton (1992) The Balanced Scorecard—measures that drive performance, *Harvard Business Review* https://hbr.org/1992/01/the-balanced-scorecard-measures-that-drive-performance-2

concerns about the impact of animal farming on climate change and an increasing concern for animal welfare. There are even more people who are not going completely vegan but are reducing meat and dairy consumption. If we went back ten years, the headlines were different. They would have been about the impact of salt and fat on heart health. But now the focus is on fibre, excess sugar and portion sizes. There has always been a demand for convenience and saving time with cooking at home for people with busy lifestyles. But this demand for convenience is being challenged by concerns about plastic use.

There are also trends created by chefs introducing new cooking styles in restaurants and people wanting to replicate these at home. Manufacturers find ways to deliver this in the supermarket in a convenient way. Indian, Thai, Mexican, Italian and Japanese foods all have enjoyed growth as people want to experiment with different foods and create variety in the home diet.

There are a lot of trends. How do we measure them? We need to be on top of trends. We need to get numbers wherever possible. Big companies hire consultants. For example, website Thefoodpeople.co.uk publishes an annual report with the trends they have spotted in the food business. We can find this information replicated in every industry. Go to an occasional conference or Google it for information, read industry reports, read the press. We must find out if we are riding the right wave.

The consideration moment

This is an area that big companies pay a lot of attention to, but smaller businesses are less attentive to. These measures are a leading indicator of how well we will do next week, next month, this year and next year:

1   Brand saliency – how many people think of our brand and recall it without being prompted by a mention of our brand name? This is top of mind awareness.

2   Brand awareness – how many people recognise our brand name and logo and have some familiarity with it when it is shown to them or they come across it? This is prompted brand awareness.

3   Brand understanding – how well do the people who have heard of our brand understand what it is, what it does and what it delivers?

4   Brand emotion – how do people who have heard of our brand feel about it, what is our likability, do they trust us, what kind of experiences have they had?

Major research firms offer brand tracking studies to help big companies understand these dimensions. Millward Brown has been one of the most successful firms offering this service. In the modern era of measurable digital marketing, these studies have become less popular. This is because marketers often feel they can measure sales lift from digital marketing campaigns and that is enough. But as we discussed in rule 5, sales activation campaigns are not enough, and we need to create brand reputation. Measuring our brand reputation gives us a prediction of the future prospects for the brand and provides guidance on what issues need to be addressed by marketing, advertising or product development. These studies also can measure the impact of marketing and advertising campaigns.

But how can we do this in a smaller business? Customised brand tracking studies are expensive. There are alternatives – Mintel, Euromonitor, Keynote and Datamonitor produce industry reports that offer quantitative data on brands and their performance along with many other customer questions. These can give us a realistic view of the market we are trying to compete in.

Here are some other suggestions that can be adopted by everyone from the brand manager at a multinational corporation to a small business start-up entrepreneur.

Brand awareness and saliency: We all live in a bubble where our brand is the centre of our working lives and it seems hard to imagine a world where no-one has heard of the brand. But unfortunately, unless we are Coca-Cola, Google, Nike, Apple, Samsung, etc., then there are many people who have yet to hear about us and many of those are in our target audience. How can we get a sense of how big our awareness is and if it is trending up or down?

- First, when people ask us what we do then pay attention to whether they had heard of our business before they met us. Is it often or rare?

- Second, look at the numbers on our website stats and social media, add up the totals that have come across us in these channels and estimate this as a percentage of our target audience. We may be shocked at how low a percentage this is. Also look at our trend data in these channels.

- Third, if the brand has some presence Google Trends will show us whether people are look-ing for our brand and whether that is going up or down. Google search our brand name to see where and how often it is mentioned.

Brand understanding: Make sure in any customer surveys we ask questions that reveal how well people understand what we offer. How do they explain it? Which statements about our service or product do they agree with?

Brand emotion: This is difficult. We can look at sentiment in social media. Tools such as SentiOne[31] can track online conversations and give us a sense of which direction we are headed in. But social media reporting is partial and often motivated by bad experiences rather than the silent majority. Emotion is difficult to measure but still vital, so we need to experiment to find what works best for us.

The purchase moment

This is easier to measure. The focus is on how easy it is for customers to find our product or service and how easy it is to transact with us and buy. There are numerous simple measures to help with this:

- number of shops where we are stocked;

- rate of sale per shop;

- number of customers buying in one month or year;

- number of websites where we are listed or linked from (plus the traffic they represent);

---

[31] https://sentione.com

- conversion rate online at each stage of the buying process.

The consumption moment

This is the whole area of customer experience and we can track this in several ways:

- customer feedback questionnaire;
- informal customer feedback;
- social media feedback;
- repeat purchase customers and frequency.

These are the stages in the customer journey:

1 the problem or need;
2 the consideration moment;
3 the purchase moment;
4 the consumption moment.

Now if we can get measures on each of these stages and we have a sense of where we are weak or strong vs where we need to be and how that is trending, then we have clarity about where to act. Most small businesses put all their effort into developing and improving number 3, the purchase moment. Then they might move onto analysing number 4 and get customer feedback. The reason is that these areas are easier to measure, and it is easier to see the immediate impact on sales.

The work by Ehrenberg, Sharp, Binet and Field shows us that we must tackle brand awareness and reputation as well as sales activation. If we only tackle number 3, the purchase moment, then we are just looking at sales activation activity and ignoring the essential task of building brand. Most successful large businesses have a balanced approach tackling all four of these stages of the customer journey. This is one of their scale advantages and means they build and defend their brand positions and smaller businesses wonder how to compete with that.

Rapidly growing small businesses that turn into large businesses also do work on brand and brand awareness; they are working on all four of these measures. Think of brands that came from nowhere and changed their markets. Innocent Smoothies, Ella's Kitchen baby food, Orange (now EE) mobile phone network, EasyJet, Jimmy's Iced Coffee, Octopus Energy, Egg Banking. They all started small and worked on brand as well as sales activation. I remember meeting Jim Cregan and he was the living big brand expression of Jimmy's Iced Coffee and hard to forget. The personality expressed in videos, social media and the brand packaging built the brand not just the sales activation.

My final suggestion is to run the numbers on how many people are aware of our business as a percentage of total target market. It is very low! The biggest growth opportunity is always to increase awareness and understanding of our brand. These new prospects will behave just like the people who encountered us in the past, some will buy, and some will not, some will like us, and some will not. But we will get more sales. Awareness is a much underrated measure.

I have a small business practical example of my own. I have a self-catering holiday house on the South Coast of England. It sleeps 10 people and is close to the beach. It is bigger than most similar accommodation in Swanage. www.purbeckholidays. co.uk. We get consistent outstanding feedback from our guests and many repeat customers. Sometimes we get periods when we are not making enough sales and have gaps in the booking calendar. The conventional industry response seems to be to discount to attract people. Many enquirers also ask for a discount. The temptation is to focus on that purchase moment and give in to the pressure. But there is a better answer. There are thousands of prospects who need the size of house we have and who live in the UK and who have not heard of us. We only need 40 customers per year. The answer is always more marketing and advertising to reach those people. Discounting is crazy given that almost everyone that stays in the house tells us we charged them a fair price, or it was good value for money. The reason we understand this is we have data on the market, our customer feedback surveys and our enquirers.

We must measure what matters and then decide where we need to act to attract more customers.

Summary

Market research can be helpful and it can be dangerous. Understand how it works and use other methods to complement it. Social media, informal customer feedback, conversations, reading the media, attending conferences can help us understand lots of things about customers and prospects. Remember that customers only look backwards at their experiences; they are not good at looking forwards. Looking forwards and imagining possibilities is our job as marketers and creators of products and services that will attract customers.

To recap, there are five rules about customers and brands. These come from the study of evidence over a 50-year period. They are not just made up or pet theories:

> *Rule 1:* Many more customers buy bigger brands than buy smaller brands and those customers buy bigger brands only slightly more often than they buy smaller brands.

> *Rule 2:* Customer loyalty is a mirage, customers are not 'loyal' in an emotional sense. They have habits. They buy our brand for as long as it suits them, when they stop buying it is either because they don't need it any more or they found an alternative that is more suited to their needs.

> *Rule 3:* Brand reputation is firstly what drives customers to buy and will determine our profitability and underpin our growth.

> *Rule 4:* Short-term sales activation effects are only short term.

> *Rule 5:* Brand building investment is essential to create long-term brand value and profit.

We must create measures that help us understand each point of the customer journey and share these with the team and the business:

1   The problem or need e.g. market trends.

2   The consideration moment e.g. brand awareness, reputation and understanding.

3   The purchase moment e.g. sales distribution and availability, website visibility and conversions.

4   The consumption moment e.g. customer feedback and social media.

But even when we create the mindset to start with the customer and we do the work to understand the customer, there are plenty of traps and pitfalls that can derail us. These are what make it so difficult to get it right. We will take a look at this in the next chapter.

Chapter 3

Why is it so difficult to get it right?

We need to convince people

First, we have to be convinced about our plan or we will not really get behind it. But then we must convince others (unless we are the only person in the business). We need people to get behind the plan. Both of these things can be difficult, even convincing ourselves, let alone the task of gaining the support and agreement from others.

Why is it so difficult to get agreement in a business to a plan? Why are we plagued by uncertainty about our plans for the brand? Why can we not convince others, even when we passionately believe we have the right plan? It can be very frustrating.

In this chapter we will explore the emotional and irrational beings that we all are. We will look at the role of randomness and chaos in determining success rather than the neat planned world we might want it to be. We will examine the influence of the opinions of the crowd, of fashionable tools and strategies. We will explore the deceptive lure of common sense and why we should be wary of it. In the summary I suggest some ways to become convinced we have the right strategy and win the support of the key people that we need to make it happen.

Randomness overrules causality and undermines predictability

The notion that systems can be designed to work, that organisations can be shaped to be effective, that smart people can make things better is hard wired into us.

For some people this notion even shapes their view of the planet and us as a species. The notion of Intelligent Design of the Earth is still fervently believed in parts of the world, notably in the USA. The idea that this world we live in was designed by an intelligent super being still holds sway.

But ever since Darwin controversially published his work *On the Origin of Species*[32] in 1859 and *The Descent of Man*[33] in 1871 we have been learning that the world is not designed, but has arisen and become the way it is through a series of evolutionary or random events. This understanding has influenced not just biology and anthropology but also affects the world of mathematics and physics as Stephen Hawking revealed in his work on black holes and the origins of the universe. [34]

In 2004 Nassim Nicholas Taleb published his work *Fooled by Randomness* and revealed his findings that success by market traders and asset managers seem to be more to do with luck than being smart. He found the same applies to CEOs of large businesses. This comes from his study

[32] Charles Darwin (1859) *On the Origin of Species,* John Murray.

[33] Charles Darwin (1871) *The Descent of Man,* John Murray.

[34] Stephen Hawking (2011) *A Brief History of Time,* Bantam.

of numbers and patterns and probability. Randomness is a better explanation of events and success than smart actions and brilliant execution.[35]

Taleb then went on to publish *The Black Swan* where he demonstrated that making predictions about what will happen in the future in markets, politics or the social world is foolish. Forecasting is a mug's game. This is because the single biggest explanation for how things turn out is random big events that were not in the official forecasts. Black Swan events are things such as 9/11, the Indian Tsunami in 2004, the run on the banks and market crash in 2008. History is littered with these, the invention of the wheel, the eruption of Pompeii, the extinction of the dinosaurs, the Great Fire of London, the Brexit vote, the Trump election. If we look back at our own lives and businesses, we will find some Black Swan events that have shaped us and shaped our businesses.[36]

Despite all this research and publishing about randomness and things operating outside of our control, we still cling to the idea that events are the result of human design and action that is good or that is bad. I personally believe that humans have clung to the notion that it is our design that determines events for three reasons. First, often we can and do design things that make our lives better, we have developed many things that make everyone's lives better e.g. clean water, healthcare, the internet, insurance, food production. Second, when things go wrong, we can analyse what happened and see the decisions and actions that led to

---

[35] Nassim Nicholas Taleb (2007) *Fooled by Randomness: The Hidden Role of Chance in Life and in the Markets,* Penguin.

[36] Nassim Nicholas Taleb (2008) *The Black Swan: The Impact of the Highly Improbable,* Penguin.

failure. Because we understand what was done wrong, we can infer there must have been a better decision and action that would have led to a different result. Third, we have an inner ego and conceit that means we believe we can make the difference, that we exist to design and make things better. Whilst that may be true and our own experiences in life reinforce this, if we apply this notion of smart human design and use it to help us understand markets, the physical and social world around us and why businesses succeed and fail, it misleads us into overrating the impact of our decisions and actions and underrating the role of randomness and luck. If we ignore the role of randomness and luck, we will not make the best decisions.

Taleb cites examples where entrepreneurs are hailed for their brilliance, when really the successful ones were just lucky. There were many who tried similar approaches and did not get as lucky. What we see in the news and media are the big successes and the spectacular failures. As ego-driven humans we look to attribute this success and failure down to people's actions rather than luck and randomness. However, one of the characteristics of lucky people is that they put themselves in the way of luck so the luck could find them. This is why the greatest characteristic of all successful entrepreneurs and other high achievers is persistence rather than brilliance. The successful people are successful because they tried more often. In fact, successful people have failed much more often than unsuccessful people, they just kept coming back. As Michael Jordan said:

> I've missed more than 9,000 shots in my career. I've lost almost 300 games. 26 times I've been trusted to take the game winning shot and missed.

I've failed over and over and over again in my life.
And that is why I succeed.[37]

We need to do the same with our brands, products and services.

Have you ever noticed in the CEO's report in the news, when things are going well it is attributed to the brilliant strategy, the hard work, the qualities of the team? When things are going badly it is down to external factors, the weather, the market, the currency, the consumers not spending. Maybe there is some understanding of randomness. Randomness explains poor performance. Human design and brilliance explains good performance!

My conclusion is that randomness overrules causality, and this makes it difficult to predict what will happen. This has certainly been my experience of launching new products and new marketing campaigns. This makes it even more important we observe the way things work and measure what is going on rather than theorise about why it happened. Our theories and explanations of how things might work are likely to be flawed. How does this apply to creating brands that will attract more customers?

First, we understand that our customers and prospects have busy lives that are subject to random events. They are not out there looking for our brand and they are unlikely to follow the customer journey outlined in our marketing strategy. The customer journey provides us with a tool to design products and marketing messages to help customers at each point of the journey. But the customer will discover these in a more random way than the journey map implies. This reinforces the discovery by Ehrenberg and Sharp

---

[37] www.virgin.com/richard-branson/failure-humility-and-celebrating-human-progress

that the first and most important thing we must do is to create brand awareness, ensure our brand is recognised and make it available and easy to buy. This is what will help us gain more customers. Byron Sharp exhorts marketers to focus on two tasks. The first he calls 'mental availability' and the second he calls 'physical availability'. If we want to benefit from this randomness, we need to be present and recognisable in the customer's mind so they can remember we exist and be present and prominent in the physical or web space so they can buy us.

Second, if we are to survive Black Swan events, we must first understand that we cannot predict them, so we cannot plan for every scenario. Instead we should create a brand and organisation that is not just strong and resilient but is what Taleb calls 'antifragile'.[38]

What is the opposite of fragile? You might say strong and resilient is the opposite. But Taleb argues this is not enough. The opposite of fragile is 'antifragile'. A fragile brand or business is vulnerable to collapse and is at the mercy of events. An 'antifragile' business is not just resilient, it is better than that, it gets stronger when subjected to stress.

This is what the Attractive Thinking process is designed to do. It will make our brand and our organisation not just stronger but 'antifragile'. By answering the five questions in the five steps PINPOINT, POSITION, PERFECT, PROMOTE and PITCH we build an organisation and brand that is focused on helping customers solve a problem and address a need. This is dynamic and responsive to customers. Our reputation and ability becomes grounded in solving that problem rather than delivering one product

---

[38] Nassim Nicholas Taleb (2012) *Antifragile: Things that Gain from Disorder*, Penguin.

or one technology or one service. Our purpose is to help customers solve that problem. This purpose is core to our brand and our organisation. That makes us 'antifragile'.

Marketers and consumers – we are not rational

This has been something that advertising creatives and marketing communicators have known for some time. Since the 1970s and earlier marketers and advertisers have tried to persuade their business colleagues that customers are emotional rather than rational beings. Finally, in the past 10 years this notion is now penetrating the business and economic world. One of the most powerful books about this is *Thinking, Fast and Slow* by Daniel Kahneman published in 2011.[39] This book took Kahneman and his colleague Amos Tversky's academic research and made it accessible to everyone. Kahneman explains how as humans we make decisions for a number of reasons, both emotional and rational, and we are subject to unconscious biases that we cannot control. Kahneman, who is a psychologist, received the Nobel Prize for Economics in 2002 for showing economists that economic decisions by humans are not all rational.

Kahneman's central thesis is that the brain has two functions. One we cannot control and one that we can. One is fast and one is slow. The one we cannot control is fast and the one we can control is slow. The fast one that we cannot control is hard wired into our system and

---

[39] Daniel Kahneman (2011) *Thinking, Fast and Slow*, Farrar, Straus and Giroux.

has evolved as slowly as Homo sapiens has evolved. It is therefore not that well attuned to the modern world in which we live. It was groomed by our history as hunter gatherers and social beings, not by our lives in cities and workplaces.

The fast one he calls System One. For example, it is the capability we have to look at a car approaching us on the road and judge whether we have time to cross the road. It is fast, automatic, frequent, emotional, stereotypic, unconscious. It allows us to see that an object is at a greater distance than another, to locate the source of a specific sound, to complete the phrase 'war and...', to display disgust when seeing a gruesome image, to solve $2 + 2 = ?$

The slow one is called System Two. It is slow, effortful, infrequent, logical, calculating, conscious. It is how we perform deliberate conscious acts such as control our behaviour in a social setting, solve 36 x 23, decide the price quality ratio between two TVs, recall and tell someone our phone number, go to the gym to get fit.

System One is subject to unconscious influences that we cannot control. Once we understand this, it helps to explain why we are not rational. Kahneman and others have identified many biases that affect our decision making. Wikipedia supplies a good list.[40] How is this relevant to creating products, services and messages that attract more customers? It affects us in two big ways.

The first and most obvious one is that customers and prospects are making buying decisions about our brand and about many other things. These decisions are influenced by behavioural and cognitive biases. If we understand these it will help us design the products and services better, position them more effectively and communicate with customers in

---

[40] https://en.wikipedia.org/wiki/List_of_cognitive_biases

a way that helps customers to respond. Richard Shotton has just published a book that explains this with colourful and easy to follow examples. His book *The Choice Factory*[41] covers 25 of the behavioural biases that influence what we buy. Rory Sutherland most eloquently explains it:[42]

> *This book is a Haynes Manual for understanding consumer behaviour. You should buy a copy – and then buy another copy to give to one of the 97% of the people in marketing who are too young to remember what a bloody Haynes Manual is.*

Here are five of the better-known biases that affect customers making a purchase:

1　The fundamental attribution error: Context matters, for example, people are more likely to buy when they are disposed to buy, have time, are not in a hurry. Whether they buy is not down to who they are or if they are the target market, it's a question of their circumstance, disposition and opportunity. Think about where and when we present ourselves to customers. Remember they are not a target trap and extract money from. The customer is a person with a problem or need that we can help to solve. They only have that need at certain times and in certain places.

2　Framing or anchoring effect: The first price someone sees for a service will set the whole context for what is good value or bad value. Brands often

---

[41]　Richard Shotton (2018) *The Choice Factory*, Harriman House.

[42]　Richard Shotton (2018) *The Choice Factory*, Harriman House.

offer a cheap, middle and premium option. Most people buy the middle one. Car manufacturers will make super premium models and will advertise those models even though the market for them is small. This helps the value perception of their mid-price models.

3   Distinction bias: This is the tendency to view two options as more dissimilar when evaluating them simultaneously than when evaluating them separately. As an example, Pepsi exploited this when they created the Pepsi Challenge. Pepsi used this to both get attention, to seem as if they are as big a brand as Coca-Cola and suggest there is a significant difference. Burger King take a similar approach to distinguishing their burgers vs McDonald's.

4   The good–bad rule: This is the tendency to fear loss more than be attracted to gain. For example, if patients are told about the risks of surgery and advised it has a 95% survival rate, they are more likely to proceed than if they are told it has a 5% death rate.

5   Social proof: People are more likely to buy things that they see other people buying. So, we queue up to go to the busy restaurant, to get the tickets for sold-out events, to fit in with the brands we are seen with. Daniel Priestley discusses how to use this bias extensively in his book *Oversubscribed*.[43]

---

[43] Daniel Priestley (2015) *Oversubscribed*, Capstone.

These biases also affect us as business decision makers and the people we need to support our plans. These unconscious biases will influence our decision making and may lead us to reject options that would be better for us and our business. Here are two of the most common ones that we need to consider.

First, familiarity bias: We will trust both people and plans that we have seen before. A quite common example of this is the way investors will tend to invest in a country they know (typically their own) or a business that they use the products of. This has little bearing on the likely success of the stock or investment but is common behaviour. It makes us feel more comfortable. It may be the right thing for the investor to do emotionally, but it is not objective.

In our business environment we will trust ideas and plans from people that we know well and feel comfortable with. We will trust ideas and plans that we have implemented before and fear those that we have not. This can be a good thing to do. What worked before will work again. But this is only true if everything is the same as it was before. Unfortunately, not everything is the same as before, not ever. Not least the fact the campaign or product may have had considerable novelty impact the first time and this novelty will not be present the second time.

This has considerable bearing on us when we make decisions; we must fight this bias if we genuinely want to come up with the best plan. It also affects us when we try to convince someone of an idea or a plan. We need to recognise how this will influence the person we are trying to convince and use this to make them feel comfortable with our plan and ideas. We look at tools to deal with this in PITCH.

Second, confirmation bias: When we see facts and evidence around us, we have an unavoidable tendency to notice the evidence that supports what we already believe.

The most obvious and extreme example of this has been evident in the Brexit debate in the UK where each side is convinced it is right and the comments in social media and national media draw selective evidence to support their case. Now this may be fine if we are trying to convince someone of our argument and we may be able to exploit this. We look at this in PITCH. But if we are trying to make the best decision then look hard at the facts and challenge ourselves to find evidence that contradicts what we want to do. That way we can be sure we are making the right decision.

In constructing our brand and our brand plan, we can exploit these biases to make our product and service and message more attractive (PROMOTE). We can use these biases to make our pitch more appealing and convincing (PITCH). But more importantly we need to look out for how these biases may cause us to make suboptimal decisions. That is where the whole Attractive Thinking process comes in. It forces us to look at five critical questions and use our best work, our most inspired creativity and the most robust evidence to answer them.

There are two more hazards that get in the way of us making the best decisions and coming up with the best ideas and plans to attract more customers. In the next two sections we will look at conventional wisdom and common sense.

The pitfalls of conventional wisdom and fashionable ideas

There is another unconscious bias that explains how conventional wisdom and the most fashionable ideas that populate the business media can lead us astray. Kahneman called it the availability heuristic. The availability heuristic is a mental shortcut that means we use the immediate examples that come to our mind when evaluating a decision. This operates on the notion that if something can be recalled, it must be important, or at least more important than alternative proposals or ideas that are not as readily remembered. People tend to use recent information to make a judgement:

> *In an experiment to test this explanation, participants listened to lists of names containing either 19 famous women and 20 less famous men or 19 famous men and 20 less famous women. Subsequently, some participants were asked to recall as many names as possible whereas others were asked to estimate whether male or female names were more frequent on the list. The names of the famous celebrities were recalled more frequently compared to those of the less famous celebrities. The majority of the participants incorrectly judged that the gender associated with more famous names had been presented more often than the gender associated with less famous names. Tversky and Kahneman argue that although the availability heuristic is an effective strategy in many situations, when judging probability use of this heuristic can lead to predictable patterns of errors.*[44]

The other influence on this bias is how much we are aware of the consequences of a decision (see discussion of 'away from' and 'towards' in PITCH). The easier it is to recall the consequences of something, the greater those consequences are often perceived to be. In other words,

---

[44] https://en.wikipedia.org/wiki/Availability_heuristic

the availability of those consequences in our minds makes us either more wary or more attracted to the action. For example, many people have a greater fear of flying than they do of driving a car even though driving a car is statistically much more dangerous. Airline accidents and terrorist incidents are much more easily recalled than car accidents (unless we had one recently). It is calculated that more people were accidentally killed on the roads in the US after 9/11 due to people refusing to fly in aircraft during the following 12 months than died in the 9/11 tragedy.

In business different people see things differently and this bias has different effects. Some can always more easily see the consequences of spending money on a product or campaign that does not work. Some of us can see the glorious future of our plan working and the revenues and profits that will flow. This frames our view of any investment decision.

The most relevant example of this bias having distorted marketers' decision making has been described by Binet and Field in their most recent IPA study *Effectiveness in Context*.[45] In this work they very convincingly demonstrate that spending has increased on short-term activation activities that are easy to measure at the expense of brand building activities that are hard to measure. They show that this trend is damaging marketing effectiveness and companies' budgets are not being as efficiently spent as previously. Businesses do not recognise the 60:40 rule about spending on brand vs activation and are drawn to spend on activities that have higher immediate consequences in creating a short-term sales lift. Binet and Field also do a detailed analysis of the 60:40 rule and show that there

---

[45] Les Binet and Peter Field (2018) *Effectiveness in Context*, IPA.

are variations to this rule in different circumstances. It can vary to 50:50 or 75:25 in favour of brand building. But it is never effective to take brand building below 50% of marketing spend.

Being drawn to and attracted to immediate and compelling consequences is the main reason digital advertising has taken off in such a dramatic way in the last ten years. Digital advertising offers this nirvana of perfect measurement and the appeal of a direct response from the customer or prospect. Digital ad spend has responded to this and became very fashionable. But there is now evidence[46] that the pendulum has swung too far[47] in favour of digital vs traditional media (print, TV, outdoor, radio).

When we are looking at how to answer the five questions in Part II, we must be careful of being attracted to the obvious answer, of being drawn to what everyone else is doing. Remember conventional wisdom and fashionable ideas are influenced by many biases. Social proof, confirmation bias, availability heuristic and the good–bad rule influence everyone. Doing what is obvious, conventional or fashionable may not be the right thing. The five questions in Attractive Thinking are designed to bring us back to the things that really matter and to flush out these unconscious biases.

It's common sense isn't it, or not? Read on.

---

[46] www.thedrum.com/opinion/2018/04/16/no-advertising-spend-not-moving-online-heres-why

[47] www.marketingweek.com/2018/12/05/mark-ritson-the-story-of-digital-media-disruption-has-run-its-course/

Challenge the deceptive power of common sense

Common sense is defined by Wikipedia as follows:[48] 'Common sense is sound practical judgment concerning everyday matters, or a basic ability to perceive, understand, and judge that is shared by ('common to') nearly all people.'

Common sense is immensely attractive and compelling and is frequently used in conversation to justify a point of view in a discussion. But science has debunked a lot of common sense. The world is flat, that common sense was challenged by Pythagoras in 2000BC but remained a common view until Ferdinand Magellan sailed around the world proving that it was not. The biggest problem with common sense is that it is subject to all the unconscious biases that we have been discussing in this book that have been amply studied by Kahneman and Tversky and many other psychologists.

The best attack on common sense was richly argued by Duncan Watts in his book. *Everything Is Obvious*: *Once You Know the Answer: How Common Sense Fails.*[49] Watts draws us to three conclusions from his analysis of common sense:

1   If we rely on common sense, we are not accounting for the cognitive biases at play.

2   Instead of trying to predict the future, stay in the present and work with what we've got.

---

[48] https://en.wikipedia.org/wiki/Common_sense

[49] Duncan Watts (2011) *Everything Is Obvious*: *Once You Know the Answer: How Common Sense Fails,* Crown Business.

3   Make better decisions by building uncommon sense, which relies on the scientific method.

We already discussed cognitive biases. We discussed randomness and Black Swans, which show that predicting the future is not reliable. What we need to do is become 'antifragile'. We discussed the scientific method looking at the work of Byron Sharp and Andrew Ehrenberg amongst others. For me, Duncan Watts' observations are bang on if we want to create a brand that will attract more customers. Be wary of common sense.

There is one bit of common sense that is often believed by business people and marketers but is not true. One of the most persuasive pillars of marketing common sense is the importance of customer loyalty. The argument goes something like this. It is much easier and cheaper to persuade an existing customer to buy again than to recruit a new customer. It makes sense to target existing customers to grow the business. There are two truths in this argument but the common sense conclusion is not backed up by empirical observation and scientific evidence. The truths are that it is easier and cheaper to communicate with an existing customer. They are already disposed to buy from us, and they are ready to listen. But the argument that they are the easiest and cheapest target market for us to sell more product is proven to be false for three reasons.

Sharp and Ehrenberg showed that people who already buy a lot in one year usually buy less the next year; the heavy buyers have no capacity to buy more. People who buy none or little are more likely to buy more. This is what happens in practice in every market. This year's heavy buyers are next year lighter and less frequent buyers. This year's light buyers or non-buyers can be persuaded to buy more next year.

Existing buyers already know us, use us and know what we can do. They are probably buying as much from us as they need. In the event we target them with a special offer, all they do is stock up in advance at the lower price and then buy less later so we have reduced our profit margin. This is exactly what happens with many brands in grocery and retail that get stuck into a promotional offer cycle that costs the company a lot, recruits only a few new buyers and gives generous discounts to existing buyers.

Binet and Field's analysis of the IPA database of marketing effectiveness award campaigns reveals that over a 25-year period some 35% of campaigns used customer loyalty as the objective and 65% of campaigns used market penetration or attracting new customers as the objective. Yet 97% of the winners used attracting new customers as their objective. Only 3% of the winners used loyalty as their objective.[50] Attracting new customers is the marketing objective that will help us create business success.

Now an awful lot of business books use an appeal to common sense and draw us in with attractive common-sense arguments. I would invite you to develop an anti-common-sense antenna and start to look for the evidence of how customers actually behave rather than the theory of how they might behave.

Summary

In Part II of this book we will look at a series of five questions that we must answer if we are to attract more customers. It adds up to a whole approach to

---

[50] Les Binet and Peter Field (2013) *The Long and the Short of It*, IPA.

developing products, services and messages that will grow the business. It is an approach founded on a belief and philosophy that being more attractive to customers is more important than extracting more money from existing customers.

This is no magic bullet; it is just the best way. It requires hard work, uncertainty and risk. In this chapter we explored why this is so difficult

First, people are not rational. Our customers do not make rational decisions to buy our products and services; they are emotional beings with unconscious biases. Our team members, investors, bosses and the board do not make rational decisions about what plan to support. We are all subject to unconscious biases.

Second, randomness and Black Swan events make it exceedingly difficult to design and predict the future. Instead we should focus on making our business and our organisation 'antifragile' and capable of withstanding and thriving on the shocks that the market will throw at us.

Third, it is tempting to follow the herd and the fashions of marketing and media wisdom. The problem with these is that they are driven by unconscious biases that lead us to like things that we have seen before and to follow things that have obviously worked for others. This bias will affect us and the people we are trying to convince.

Fourth, common sense can distract us from the thing that is most effective. We need to look at the science and evidence of customer behaviour to avoid common sense.

We have looked at four themes that are critical if we want a brand strategy that everyone is convinced will work.

In the Introduction and in Part I, we looked at:

1   Why attraction matters: Attracting is better than extracting and why that works.

2   Start with the customer: Why and how to get a customer mindset, the fundamentals of creating value for your customers that will attract them to your brand and business.

3   How to understand customers: Where does market research fit in, what you can ask customers and rules that govern how customers actually behave; what we should be measuring and how to get them accepted by ourselves and everyone else.

4   Why is it so difficult to get it right?: People are not rational, events are often random and unexpected, don't follow the herd, understand the unconscious biases and be wary of common sense.

Now we are ready to go to Part II, examine the five fundamental questions and explore how to answer them. At the end of this we will have a plan to attract more customers to your brand and everyone will be convinced the plan will work.

Part II
How to apply
Attractive Thinking

Chapter 4

The five questions and why

Attractive Thinking is about providing something that is just what the customer needs at that time. This something will solve a customer's problem or address their need. This is the defining purpose of our brand and business. If we can do this then the marketing task is remarkably simple. All the marketer has to do is let people know about it. All sales and distribution need to do is to make it available and easy to buy. The image earlier in the book showing the final piece of the jigsaw illustrates our role as creators and marketers.

Attractive Thinking considers the brand and the customer are working together. The brand is there to serve the customer not to exploit them. Brands that mange to do this attract more customers and grow faster. If the business is well run, it makes a profit. Without profit the business will not be able to invest in the product and service, then it will stop serving the customer and it will attract fewer customers. Profit is intrinsic to Attractive Thinking. But extracting profit from customers is not our start point. The start point is solving the problem for the customer.

The opposite is Extractive Thinking. This starts with making a profit. The premise is that business is about making as much profit from customers as possible. However, this sets up an immediate tension between the brand and the customer, since the brand is trying to get something from the customer rather than trying to offer them something to help them. This extractive approach is summed up by the cowboy image with the lasso used earlier in the book.

In this extractive environment marketing is out to get customers, to keep customers (even to trap customers in contracts). Product and service design is about reducing all costs that we can get away with. Marketing comprises tricks and devices such as advertising that over promises, introductory discounts to lure people in, endless re-marketing adverts for something the customer already bought. Sales and distribution make the customer feel badgered either in-store or online.

Attractive Thinking, in contrast, makes life much simpler and a lot more fun and we attract more customers. We can get away from tricks and manipulative tactics. Another feature of Attractive Thinking is to stop using elaborate brand and marketing language and talk in straight forward language that everyone will understand. Remember we are providing something that is just what the customer needs at that time. Then all the marketing has to do is let people know about it. All the sales and distribution need to do is to make it available and easy to buy. It will be easier to engage the team in the business since everyone will feel they are doing something worthwhile. This is motivating. And finally, with this approach it will be easier for us as creators and marketers to pitch the plan to investors, the board or the boss because they will see the opportunity and understand what we are doing.

The Attractive Thinking approach requires us to answer five questions. The questions are:

1   Who are our customers and what are their problems?

2   How can we solve their problem and stand out?

3   How do we create a product or service that delivers this?

4   How do customers find out about it and where do they buy it?

5   How do we engage our shareholders, board directors, colleagues and customers?

Each question becomes a step of the Attractive Thinking process. Each step has a name. These are shown in Figure 4.1. The subtitle of this book is: The five questions that drive

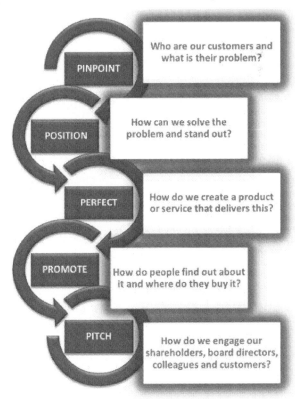

Figure 4.1 The five questions

successful brand strategy and how to answer them. So far, I have tried to set out why these are the five questions that we must answer. Now we move on to how to answer them.

As we get into the next five chapters, I would ask you to suspend scepticism and lean in. Trust the process. Each step is designed to be quite straightforward. The questions are not trick questions, they are simple. There are five steps. We use research, analytics and workshops as part of every step. I will show different ways we can approach this. The first step is an intuitive 'entrepreneurial' approach. The second step uses workshops and analysis, which needs time and commitment. The third step uses advanced analytics that take more time and cost more money.

Each step requires three activities to get to the answer:

1   Research: To generate insight about customers, list possible answers to the question, create ideas on what we could do.

2   Analysis: To get clarity about which options are likely to work best, which are the areas we should focus on.

3   Workshops and consultations: To get agreement in the team that we have the right answer, to make sense of the analytics, to improve on the answers.

Chapter 5

PINPOINT

Who are our customers and what are their problems?

Let me start with some signposting of what this is about. In a marketing textbook this chapter would be called 'defining your target market'. However, I think we need new language to replace this idea of a target. If you look up the *Oxford English Dictionary* definition of target, you will find: 'target: a person, object, or place selected as the aim of an attack'. There are three secondary definitions for target that are not really any more appealing: 'target: a mark or point at which one fires or aims. target: an objective or result towards which efforts are directed. target: a person or thing against whom criticism or abuse is directed.'

The notion of a target suffers two problems. First, the language really fits better with Extractive Thinking where we are aiming at people, we are targeting people to get something from them. Second, it is potentially very limiting and will reduce our growth. Later in this chapter, we will look at how limiting ourselves to a target that is too narrow can damage sales. However determined we are to sell to a defined target market, some off-target customers will still buy it. We need to recognise this in our marketing and selling. Changing the language is one step to help that.

In this chapter we will explore how to define the audience of prospects and customers we want to attract. This will cover defining the markets where we choose to compete, describing our customers and prospects and identifying the problems they have that we can solve. We will then PINPOINT which of these markets, customers and problems are the ones where our brand is most likely to succeed.

Define our market(s), make a list

Before we answer the question 'who are our customers and what are their problems?', we need to define the product or service market we are considering. If we have just one market and we all agree on it then this will not take long. To give you some idea of what I mean by a market, here are some examples of definitions of a market that I have worked with:

- Boxes of chocolates suitable for casual gifting and sharing e.g. Celebrations, Galaxy Jewels.

- Snack bars that keep me going between meals e.g. Snickers, Kit Kat, Eat Natural.

- Products that make it easier to look after my garden e.g. Miracle-Gro, Weedol, Evergreen, Westland.

- Legal conveyancing services that enable me to buy or sell a property e.g. Fridays Move, the local solicitor.

- Catering services providing canteens, dining, catering in offices and at events e.g. Aramark, Sodexo.

- Soft drinks supply to the food service business e.g. PepsiCo, Britvic.

- Mortgages to help people buy a home for themselves e.g. Nationwide, Santander, Britannia.

- Savoury snacks to have with your lunch, on the go or with drinks e.g. Kettle Chips, Tyrells Crisps.

- Satisfying milk drinks to keep you going or as meal replacement e.g. Mars, Yazoo.

- Convenient desserts in pots to have at home, on the go or with lunch e.g. mousses, trifles, yoghurts.

- Recruitment agencies providing flexible project workers in an industry e.g. oil and gas.

- Reinsurance brokers helping retail insurers offset their risk book by sourcing insurance capital providers e.g. AON Benfield.

- Ales sold on tap in pubs e.g. Caffrey's, Boddingtons, John Smith's.

To ask the question 'who are our customers and what are their problems?', we need to start with a definition of our product or service market. In smaller businesses this is a quick process that takes a 15–30-minute discussion and we will find we are operating in one or, at most, two markets. But we should still have that discussion to see if everyone in the team agrees that is what we are doing. If we have access to market research reports on our industry or that we have done ourselves in the business then we should read these as it will inform our decision.

However, in a larger business we often find that the business is competing in several different markets. The business has a list of these markets that it is operating in and there can be a debate about which of these markets offers the greatest opportunity to attract customers and get more growth. A simple example at Scotts Miracle-Gro, they operate in several gardening product categories such as:

- Compost to fill pots on the patio and renew the beds and borders in the garden e.g. Scotts Miracle-Gro.

- Plant foods that encourage growth e.g. Miracle-Gro.

- Weed killers that help maintain patios, borders and lawns e.g. Weedol.

- Lawn care that nourishes and greens the lawns e.g. Evergreen.

The business pursues all of them, but at different times the team chooses different priorities for investment. It is important the team has a way to agree this.

As a business, if we have more than one product or service market where we compete or would like to compete then we will have to make choices. There may also be markets that do not exist, but we believe we can create. Spectacular examples of new categories created by new businesses are:

- Streaming video services e.g. Netflix.

- Phones that also have internet and camera e.g. iPhone.

- Apps on iPhones and Android.

- Point to point cheap flights that anyone can book and change easily e.g. EasyJet.

Here are examples where businesses created new markets with new customers and new buying occasions and needs:

- The continuous reinvention of on-the-go lunch food in cities and travel destinations e.g. Pret, Eat, Itsu, Leon.

- Smart TVs that stream internet TV and games e.g. Samsung.

- Making chocolate gift giving acceptable and fun by miniaturising popular brands e.g. Celebrations.

- Recruitment agencies reinventing themselves as stable regular employers of flexible short-term staff.

- Mortgage providers providing loans on a buy to holiday let basis e.g. Principality.

At this stage the task is simple, make that list of existing and new markets and categories where we want to compete. This will be based on what our business does or would like to do.

Now we have defined the markets where we wish to compete. If we have several markets or categories we want to compete in but do not have the time or money to address all of them then we must make choices from that list. The analytics later in this chapter will help us do that.

Who are our customers? Describe them, make a list

There are lots of different ways to define different types of people. Here some generic ones we often see being used:

Age	Class	Life stage	Usage frequency
16–24	A	Screenies	Weekly
25–34	B	Generation Z	Monthly
35–44	C1	Millennials	Quarterly
45–54	C2	Generation X	Once a year
55–64	D	Boomers	< Once a year
65+	E		Never used

The advantage of these definitions is that we can get data on these classifications from published research reports. The disadvantage is that these definitions do not reflect how people see themselves. They do not give us insight into 'who are our customers?'. We need a different way to describe our customers. One that does give us insight into what they are like.

A quick way is to get a small group of us who know about the business and our customers to sit down round a table. Each person comes up with their list and writes them on separate large sticky notes. Then we share our list with everyone else by sticking them on a board, so we all look at them together. Usually each person will come up with five to ten different types of customers. Some of us will produce similar or identical types. We can group these similar ones into clusters. If we have access to market research reports on our industry or research that we have done ourselves then we should get the group to read those in advance of holding this short group workshop.

Figure 5.1 is an example of a board looking at customers of a wholesale fabric supplier to the garment trade. In this example we split the list into type of company and role of person within that company. This distinction is particularly important in B2B. It is not the business (e.g. Topshop) that buys, it is always specific people that buy (a buyer or designer), so our list needs to describe those people and understand their issues and frustrations. We need to solve these people's practical (e.g. timetable) and emotional problems (e.g. frustration) not some abstract idea of the business problem. Any list in B2B must describe individuals inside the businesses that we aim to help. Here is an example from the fabrics business:

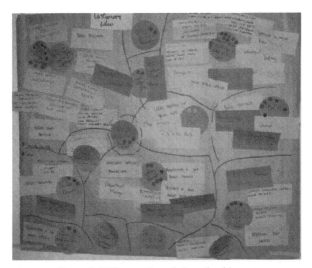

Figure 5.1 Photo of workshop looking at
customers of a fabric supplier

Retail chains/store groups: Asos, Topshop, River Island

Director decision maker

Fabric sourcer

Brand managers

Merchandiser

Departmental buyers

Designers

Giant store groups: Tesco, Walmart, Zara, Next

Director decision maker

Fabric sourcer

Brand managers

Merchandiser

Designers

Departmental buyers

Manufacturers and suppliers to retail chains

Business owner

Designer

Technologist tester

Brand owners/couture

Owners

Designers

Sourcing agents

Here are some examples of B2B customers from another list. This is for a catering company providing canteens, restaurants, events and fine dining to different types of businesses:

Traditional factory site with canteen

Multi-tenant site or co-working space

9–5 administrative workplace

Progressive meritocratic organisation that wants to reward staff

Individualistic work style, flexible creative types

Creative and media industries

Public services (government premises)

Highly educated (political and social) e.g. universities

This list of business types was also complemented by a list of the people in each firm that the caterer needs to serve and consider:

On-site manager for food and beverage services

CEO and the board

HR team

Staff who eat in the canteens and restaurants

Finance director

Chefs

Here is a sample from another list for a sales training consultancy looking at small business owners in need of sales training. Here the person is always 'the small business owner':

Any business up to £5m

People who are scared of selling/don't like it

Decision makers who run a business

People who feel that they could do better at sales

People who are comfortable with technology

People who have identified a sales skill gap in their business

People who are motivated to take action

If we do this exercise, we will have a customer list. We just read our previous research, held a short workshop, asked a simple question to a small group of people who know our business and then made a list of the different types of customer we can serve. That is all. The criteria and segmentation of the list does not matter that much. It just needs to make sense to us. These intuitive segmentations of customers are more insightful than the official ones held in market research data banks. Remember if we are doing this in B2B we must identify the individual people that buy and not just the functions and roles that they have. Our descriptions must describe them.

In the next step we are going to use this to generate insight about what problems our customers have and how we can help them address those problems.

What are our customers' problems? Describe them, make a list

The process to generate a list is the same as the one described in 'who are our customers?' above. What do we mean by customers' problems? These are not problems with the product, brand or service such as it does not work, it does not taste good, the instructions did not work. This is not about customer satisfaction or dissatisfaction with the product or service. This about problems and issues that our customers have in their daily personal, business and social lives that they would like to get some help with. Why does this matter to us as creators and marketers of products, brands and services? Because no-one ever bought anything from anyone unless they had a problem that they needed to solve. None of us stick our hands in our pockets to buy a brand just because we like the brand or the salesperson. Liking the brand or person will influence which brand we buy. But we only buy when we have a problem to solve or need to address.

When we go to the supermarket, we do not have a list of brands we are going to buy, what we have is a list of occasions and events that we need groceries and food for. Some of that is a list of essentials that we need to solve problems in the house, dishwasher tablets, washing powder, toothpaste, cleaning materials. Some of it is a list of events and things that will happen, family meals, kids coming home from school hungry, packed lunches, friends coming round, going away travelling, breakfast, lunch and dinner, moments when we want indulgences and treats. We go around the store looking for the best options to fulfil these occasions. An unfulfilled need is a problem that we need to solve.

In high-end business services, no buyer ever puts out a tender or a call to a supplier unless there is something they cannot get done in the business. They have a problem they need to solve. I have personal experience of selling high-end consultancy services. I never got any work by calling someone or writing to them. Contracts and business arise when they call me. When the client is short of insight or resources to develop their brand or create new products, if they knew me before they pick up the phone or send an email. It is that simple. And it is never different from that.

In Chapter 1 we talked about starting with the customer not with the brand. Understanding the customer's problems is the best way to start with the customer. The answer to this question defines our business purpose, what our brand stands for and who our competitors are. These are the questions I ask when people ask me for advice about their brand:

1   Who do you send invoices to? This is another version of the question 'who are your customers?'. Sometimes people describe their business in a way that means I have no idea what they sell to whom. This question cuts through to answer this.

2   What kind of business or personal problems do you help them solve? This tries to get the person to think in a customer mindset rather than a supplier mindset. This works best if the person can get inside the customer's mind.

For us to develop our brand we need to understand what problems our customers have that we can help them with. We need to create a list. We use the same process as the previous question. Here are some examples of customer problem lists from work I have done.

The first one is a photo of a board we did to look at the problems skiers have with their ski trips and the frustrations they might experience once they arrive at the resort (Figure 5.2). This produced this list of skier problems to select from and work out how we can provide a better service in the resort:

Figure 5.2 Board exploring problems faced by skiers

List of skier problems

Where and when are the lift queues?

Is my skiing good enough to go off-piste?

How to find the right runs for my group?

What is the weather forecast for today?

Where is it safe to go off-piste?

What are the snow conditions like?

Where will I find the best snow?

Where are we going to stop for lunch?

Can I find some nice quiet runs?

How can I improve my skiing technique?

What time do lifts close?

How to look after the kids and enjoy my skiing?

How cold is it today, how many layers?

Where should I go to hire skis?

What are the best ski runs to do today?

How can I get an instructor that will give me a good time?

What other non-skiing activities are there for non-skiers?

Which bars are good for après?

Here is a sample from another list that we created to express the problems and needs people have that lead them to donate to a charity or cause:

List of problems and needs that cause people to donate to a charity

I want to leave my mark with a legacy.

I have a duty to support a charity.

I want to honour and pay back those who served the country.

Giving to a deserving cause makes me feel better.

I want to make a difference and have an impact.

Helps me fit in with a current trend.

We want to enhance our image as an organisation.

Helps me network and meet more people.

I want to create awareness for my business or cause.

I want to commemorate a loved one.

I like to support my family and friends when they ask.

I need a motive to participate in events to get fitter.

Looking for a focus to create social activity for me.

I need to feel involved with local community.

I need to give the money away.

Here is another list of problems that might cause people to consume digestive or plain biscuits. The problems and needs revolve around occasions, times of day, social events and physical need:

List of problems and needs that cause people to consume plain biscuits

Friends are coming round, I offer a drink, plus a biscuit makes it more special.

Offering a biscuit creates a relaxed environment for a chat (home/office).

Work teams need a break, providing biscuits in the office shows care.

Need something to go with my cheese at lunch, dinner or snack.

Satisfies me when I am hungry, a bit peckish.

Convenient daily goodness provides an energy boost.

Provides texture contrast in my lunchbox (is a bit boring).

Want some bread but have not got any (clean tasting texture/eat).

Travelling snack when in car, train, plane.

Cheer up team after sport – team leader.

Brings etiquette to the tea break (better tea breaks).

> Student cheap rewarding wholesome calories.
>
> I need a break when on my own at home or at the office.

We must pay close attention to the way these problems are written. They should not be written as short words and phrases such as 'poor quality' or 'communication', they must be specific and detailed. They are also written from the perspective of the customer, often written in the first person. This style makes them seem real and makes them more powerful as tools to help us develop a better and more attractive brand.

This approach works equally well in high-end B2B as in consumer brands. In B2B it is always a person or a team of people buying. We have to find out what their problems are and ensure our brand is seen to help them with their problems both personal, relationships, financial and business. The method I have described here will help us think about the person who is buying and not just the business that they work for.

Now we have three lists:

1   The markets in which we operate or might enter.

2   Who are our customers?

3   What are their problems?

The next step is to analyse these and identify which of these groups we are best equipped to serve. The analytics will answer this for us.

Which markets, customer types and problems are we best equipped to serve?

We need to select the best opportunities for us from each of the three lists of market segments:

1   The market we wish to compete in.

2   The five types of customers we wish to serve.

3   The five problems we are best equipped to solve.

I will first describe the analytics method then show some spreadsheet tools that we can use and suggest an intuitive way we can make a selection.

To start the analytics, we will assess each segment against five scoring criteria. These criteria are derived from what every entrepreneur, senior manager, board director and CEO talks about when they are describing an opportunity and explaining why it is such a good opportunity for the business. You might have heard phrases like this:

- It is a big market.

- The market is growing really fast, we should get in there and ride the wave.

- This is a very profitable segment, people will pay a premium for this.

- We have a real advantage in this market segment.

- No-one is really doing a good job here; I think we could do better than the existing players.

We can translate these phrases into these five scoring criteria. I have grouped them under two headings:

Size of opportunity

How big is this segment?

Is the segment growing or declining in size?

Is this segment willing to pay a premium?

Competitive gap in the market

Can we deliver to this segment with competitive advantage?

Are the needs of this segment currently satisfied or unsatisfied?

Figure 5.3 shows how we use the criteria and run analytics that will PINPOINT the answer to the question 'who are our customers and what are their problems?'.

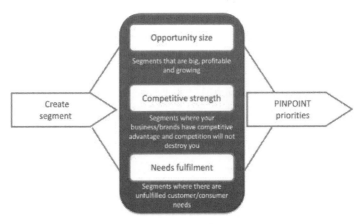

Figure 5.3 The PINPOINT analytics

The best method is to have the scoring done by five or six people each working individually and then consolidate the data from everyone. This removes individual bias and creates a score based on the 'wisdom of crowds'.[51] The collective wisdom of a qualified group is way superior to any one person's point of view. A qualified group comprises people who understand something about customers, the business and are committed to the process to get the right answer. Then plot the scores for size of opportunity and competitive gap on a bubble chart that places each segment in one of four quadrants. We can do this for the customer list (see Figure 5.4).

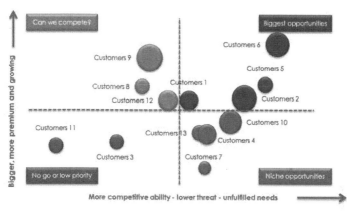

Figure 5.4 Bubble chart of who are our customers

We can also do this for the problem list (and the markets list if we have one) – see Figure 5.5.

---

[51] James Surowiecki (2004) *Wisdom of Crowds*, Doubleday; Anchor.

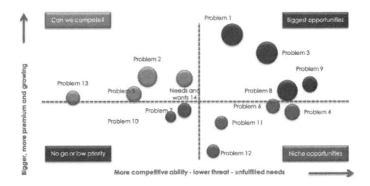

Figure 5.5 Bubble chart of what are their problems

We can then start to select the segments that are the opportunities we wish to pursue. From this we make a choice of one market and five segments from each list that are the most promising segments for the business to attract more customers. Figure 5.6 summarises it.

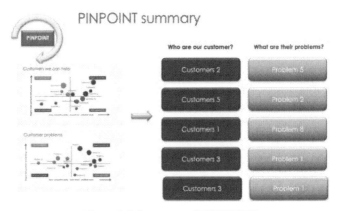

Figure 5.6 Summary of PINPOINT

Now we have PINPOINTed the most attractive opportunities for the business and brand, and we have answered the question: Who are our customers and what are their problems?

The aim here is to have a list of five customer types and five customer problems that we are best equipped to address. How to do this? There is not enough room in the book to do this for the graphics and charts shown here but in summary:

1   Make an intuitive judgement from the lists of customers and problems that we generated earlier. This is best done in groups of three to four people looking at them together and making choices by thinking through the five criteria.

2   Run the analytics using the spreadsheet tools and instructions. You can get access to these at https://chrisradford.net/attractive-thinking/. This will work if there is someone with good experience of Microsoft Excel and who is familiar with manipulating the graph functions in Excel. We can get the input for the spreadsheets by collecting scores from several people or just sitting down with a colleague and scoring each item on each list.

3   Hire some help. You can go to www.differentiate.co to see how my consultancy delivers this.

What really matters for Attractive Thinking is that we can answer the question 'who are our customers and what are their problems?' and that we are convinced it is the right answer. All creators and marketers make decisions about this when they create a product, service and marketing message. So it is better to do it as well as we can and be sure we all agree we have the best answer for our business.

In my personal experience, some entrepreneurial and creative people will prefer to generate the list of possible answers and then pick out the best options themselves using gut instinct. Some people will prefer to follow the analytical process to get the answer. The great thing is that the answer from the analytics seems blindingly obvious when we see it for the first time and it makes perfect sense. Then we wonder why we could not see it so clearly before we ran the process. Well, we could not see before and now we can, that is good enough for me. In fact, if the answer seems odd and does not make sense, then I query the process and go back to check where we might have made a mistake.

Should we go niche to focus on one customer type and one problem or go wider?

Byron Sharp controversially states that segmentation is a waste of marketers' time and that as marketers we should seek to attract the whole market for our products. Instead we must work on building memorable branding and use this to create mental availability and physical availability for customers. The core of this argument is that it is more important to be noticed by and available to everyone that might buy than to restrict our marketing to segments that are more likely to buy. Marketers' efforts should be directed to developing memorable and noticeable brand icons and ensuring these are as visible as possible to get recognition and be noticed. Then we must create physical availability making the brand easy to notice and easy to buy. If as marketers we restrict our efforts just to the heaviest buyers and the people most likely to buy, we limit our market potential and damage our growth because attracting light buyers is important for us to achieve growth.

Byron Sharp cites a dramatic case study that contrasted McDonald's vs Burger King.[52] Burger King chose to advertise to its core demographic of young men, whilst McDonald's sought to broaden its appeal to everyone. Sharp shows how and why Burger King suffered severe losses of market share as a result of this strategy.

This finding seems to be at odds with a frequent observation that when a business specialises in one audience, it becomes much more attractive to that audience than a business that does not specialise. For example, some accountants might be choosing a marketing agency. They find one that seems smart, but this agency says they work for different businesses in various markets, so they have an accountancy client and a law firm client and an estate agency client. Then another agency says, we only work for accountancy firms, we have five great clients, we really understand your marketing requirements. The accountancy firm is more likely to choose the second firm that specialises.

Now these two points do not contradict each other. Both observations are correct. The answer lies in how we answer the question about which market we operate in. The problem for Burger King was that its customer base was much broader than young men; they also served women, older people, families etc. As a result of their advertising they lost many customers who were not young men. Their business model depended on attracting a broad market; their advertising was only

---

[52] Byron Sharp (2012) *Marketing: Theory, Evidence, Practice*, Oxford University Press.

relevant to 25% of their customers who accounted for 40% of their sales. In the marketing agency example, the agency can decide it will only sell to accountants. They know that limits their market, but they have decided that the market is big enough for them and they would rather be competitive in that market by showing they are expert specialists.

Byron Sharp is right, we must define and describe our whole market and ensure our marketing reaches out to all of them. We must not be too restrictive. The exercises I have described here are to help us describe our market and understand it. These are the decisions we are trying to make:

1   Which market are we seeking to attract, create or enter? This is a decision that defines our business.

2   Who are our customers? Do not restrict this but do understand which markets we must tackle first.

3   What are our customers' problems and needs? This will help us design the best product, service and message to attract customers.

Of all these questions we must answer, the one that is most important is 'what are our customers' problems and needs?'. Because anyone that has that problem or need is a potential customer and it does not really matter who they are. We must find problems and needs that are real for real people and that have an emotional element. This applies equally in B2B and consumer brands and markets.

Now we have done PINPOINT we have answered the first Attractive Thinking question and we know who our customers are and what their problems are. We can move on to answer the second of our five questions.

Chapter 6

POSITION

How can we solve the problem and stand out?

Customers have choices about how to solve their problems

In PINPOINT we crystallised who are the customers and what are their problems. Here are some examples from different markets that describe a problem that customers want to solve.

Toothpaste

I don't want to change my diet but want to protect my teeth from decay.

My teeth are sensitive, I want to protect them so I can enjoy ice cream, cold and hot drinks without pain.

My gums are bleeding and receding, I am not good at flossing, I want protection that heals the gum disease and protects my gums.

Catering services purchased by the facilities manager

People want delicious fresh cooked locally sourced food but are not willing to pay the full cost of delivering that.

Certifying and testing consumer technology products

Certification is a big hurdle to get over. It is expensive and time consuming. It slows down my time to market. The cost restricts the number of products I can bring to market. Testing takes longer than I think it should. I am worried that the product will fail the test, which would jeopardise my launch.

Gardens and patios

I have people coming round for a barbecue, I want the patio and garden to look nice, but I don't have the time or knowledge to fix this.

Estate Agents working with conveyancing solicitors

The longer it takes to close the deal, the more likely it is that the deal will fall over, and I will not get paid. I need the legal work done fast.

In PINPOINT we defined our customers' problems. But now we must consider all the choices the customer has to solve their problem. That leads us to three questions:

1   Which alternatives can the customer choose from to solve this problem (our competitors)?

2   What do our competitors offer to solve this problem?

3   What is it that we do that solves this problem better than or as well as the alternatives?

It is the problem we solve that defines the market we are in. The customer in the supermarket is thinking about the meals they are going to have to prepare and the guests or family they need to cater for. The technology products firm is focused on getting its product to market and the hurdles they must overcome. The customers are looking for the familiar and for new inspiration. They are often not looking for our brand. We are just one of the alternatives. Our next task is to generate a list of all the other ways our customers could solve their problem in addition to the ways our product can help them.

Be distinctive and relevant

Al Ries and Jack Trout published a marketing classic in 2001 called *Positioning: The Battle for Your Mind* and Jack Trout followed this up with *Differentiate or Die* in the same year.[53] These books emphasise that in an era when there are 40,000 products in a supermarket and the internet is throwing up even more choice, the challenge is how to stand out. Trout produces compelling case studies

---

[53] Al Ries and Jack Trout (2001) *Positioning, The Battle for Your Mind*, McGraw Hill. Jack Trout (2001) *Differentiate or Die: Survival in Our Era of Killer Competition*, Wiley and Sons.

and draws several conclusions. Price is not an effective or profitable differentiator, neither is offering a very wide range of products. Instead he invites us to find out what matters to customers and is unique to our product or service and make that the central point of our brand positioning. This is known as the unique selling proposition (USP). This is the differentiating point. This is how to stand out.

But, and it is a big but, only if it is noticed and relevant. Byron Sharp has challenged this very appealing theory with his understanding of how customers actually behave. If we go into a supermarket, we do not pay attention to 40,000 products, we only notice a few. We also do not give that much consideration to our choices, often just choosing the one we had last time. Those few that we notice are likely to be things we have bought before (our repertoire) or things that stand out due to advertising, packaging, display or promotion in store. Inevitably we end up choosing from the ones we notice and ignore the ones we do not notice. This implies we must focus on three priority tasks:

1 Branding: Be easy to recognise and easy to understand what we offer.

2 Mental availability: Be in the customer's mind at the time of their need.

3 Physical availability: Be available and easy to buy at the moment of need.

What does that require us to do?

1 Branding: Have recognisable, distinctive, memorable brand logos, images, colours, memory triggers.

2 Mental availability: Advertise, PR, news, keep reminding customers we exist, they find it easy to forget.

3 Physical availability: In store, on search engine, on website, social media, be there and be easy to buy.

Attractive Thinking argues that Byron Sharp is right but that the branding is not just about being distinctive and memorable (these are essential) but also about being relevant. To be relevant we need to be known for solving the problem or need that the customer has and we need to be liked by the customer. Being liked is a function of how we leave the customer feeling as a result of having an experience with our brand. In this POSITION chapter we are working on three critical questions to create our brand strategy. This is our BRAND CORE:

- What do we do?

- What are we known for?

- How do we leave people feeling?

We will come on to creating distinctiveness, awareness and memorability in the PERFECT and PROMOTE chapters.

Some questions we can ask our customers

In the search to be relevant we need to find out what really matters to customers when they are looking for something to solve their problem. This is something we should not purely guess at, but we should ask our customer. We can ask our customers a variant of this question:

> When you are looking to buy something that helps you do xxx, which of these attributes of a product or service is more or less important to you in choosing between options?
>
> Here are 25 different attributes that you might consider. Please choose the 10 that are most important to you and then rank those 10 from 1 to 10 where 1 is the most important and 10 is the least important.

To be able to ask this question we need to come up with a list of attributes. So, what do we mean by attribute? An attribute is feature or benefit of a brand that a customer perceives it possesses or delivers. Here are some example attributes from four different types of businesses. They are printed in alphabetical order with no significance attached to the order. Take a look at the way they are written. They are an expression of how the customer might see what the business does.

This example contains attributes for a provider of safety and certification services to manufacturers of consumer technology products. Here are a few examples of attributes they might possess in the mind of the customer:

> Actively helps me solve technical problems.
>
> Adapts their service level to get to the price I need.
>
> Can provide testing when I need it, even at short notice.

Creates a bespoke test plan to deliver exactly what I need.

Delivers test results fast that meet my timetable.

Ensures I can access someone who sorts out problems quickly.

Has engineers who understand my products/technical needs.

Has support located near me and in my language.

Is a leader who stays ahead in the industry.

Is a one-stop shop – provides all the services I need.

Keeps me up to date with regulatory/certification requirements.

Provides accurate quotes quickly with no unnecessary delays.

Understands my problems and listens to my needs.

This example shows attributes for an estate agent selecting a legal conveyancing service to which to refer clients. Here are some example attributes of the conveyancing service:

Always attends to my deal.

Foresees and solves problems.

Gets instructed quickly by client.

Has experience and knowledge.

Has up to date online status file.

I can always deal with the person I know.

Offers my client no sale no fee.

Pays me a good referral fee.

Proficient at conveyancing work.

Takes responsibility and is proactive.

Takes time to explain issues.

Tips me off when there's a problem.

We work well together.

Will get deal done quickly.

This example lists some attributes that a consumer might consider when choosing between chilled fruity desserts. Here are some examples of attributes for fruity desserts:

Can get all layers in one mouthful.

Can get right pack size for my family (e.g. large, 4pk, 2pk).

Can place pack directly on table – is presentable.

Can reseal the pack/lid so can put back in fridge.

Cream is real and fresh not squirty or artificial.

Each ingredient has authentic taste (e.g. real custard, fruit, sherry).

Firm texture (does not collapse when I put my spoon in).

Fulfilling and satisfying to eat (feel like I've had enough).

Has good shelf life (lasts a few days in my fridge).

Has recyclable packaging – is environmentally friendly.

Robust packaging protects product so looks great when gets home.

Tastes, looks and smells fresh not artificial when I open it.

Uses only natural and good quality ingredients.

This example list of attributes is from a consumer choosing digestive and plain biscuits:

After eating, it leaves you feeling good, you are glad you ate it.

Baked slower and for longer to develop better taste.

By choosing this better product it shows I thought about my friends and the time we spend together.

Does not fill me up so I can still eat my meals.

Does not make me feel too guilty after eating it.

Has a strong flavour.

Has the right level of sweetness, not too much, but still tastes great.

I can dunk it in my hot drink.

I can see and know where the ingredients come from.

Is hand processed in batches with care not mass produced.

Leaves a clean, appealing taste in the mouth – no bad aftertaste.

Made by a small company that cares about quality and taste not just cost and profit.

Made with wholemeal or wholegrain flour so it is better for me.

Only uses simple ingredients that I can recognise and understand.

Pack feels and looks beautiful – shows everyone it is a better product so they know it will taste good.

Uses proper ingredients and an authentic recipe for better taste.

The first step in POSITION is for us to produce this list for our product and service category. Our list will express everything a customer might consider. We should describe an attribute with rich language and make it as evocative as possible. Attributes can be functional or emotional.

There are two methods to produce the list. The first is just like in PINPOINT, hold a small workshop with the business team, get everyone to write down all the possibilities onto separate sticky notes. Then share them with each other by sticking them up on a board and clustering them into groups with similar attributes. There are a few different questions we can ask and things we can do to produce ideas for attributes:

- Describe all the features and benefits of our product.

- Look at websites and products of competitors.

- Look at social media commentary.

- Look at competitor advertising.

- Ask the question what would an ideal xxxxx deliver and do?

- Ask the question what really matters to customers about our product and our competitor's product?

Now we have the list of attributes we can subject them to some analytics to work out which of these attributes are the POWER DRIVERS. This is what will make us be relevant and stand out.

Get clarity with analytics

Here are the analytics to understand the POWER DRIVERS that will ensure our brand is relevant and stands out. It works as shown in Figure 6.1.

Figure 6.1 POWER DRIVER analytics

The four criteria are:

1 Importance: What is it about the product or service that matters most to customers when they are choosing which brand to buy?

2 Uniqueness: How many other brands also deliver this attribute, so how differentiating is the attribute, does it offer us potential to stand out?

3 Credibility: If we say we offer this, will customers find it credible, will they believe we can do it well?

4 Competitiveness: Are we really better at this than the competitors, can we deliver this attribute and can we do it for a reasonable cost?

There are two types of power for a POWER DRIVER:

1 Market power: This fuses importance and uniqueness scores for each attribute. The highest scores indicate potential POWER DRIVERS for any brand seeking to compete in the market.

2 Brand power: This fuses credibility and competitiveness and shows us which POWER DRIVERS will work best for our brand.

Almost all the real-world examples I have come from client work and to reveal them would breach confidentiality agreements. But I have two projects we did with real research with real consumers that I can use as examples.

Example 1: Biscuits
This was a study into plain digestive biscuits and whether it would be practical to position a new product against

McVitie's. This was to be in response to McVitie's removing ingredients to make the product seem less unhealthy and to save money.

We conducted consumer research and applied the POWER DRIVER analytics. The results are shown in four types:

- Hot attributes are potentially powerful to attract consumers to buy the product.

- Warm attributes are a bit less powerful.

- Cool attributes are even less powerful.

- Cold attributes are not at all effective in attracting people to buy a product.

The full list of attributes that we considered relevant to biscuits is shown in Figure 6.2.

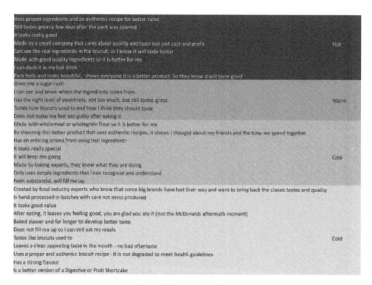

Figure 6.2 Generating attributes for biscuits in workshop

From this we developed a summary of what an ideal new product would offer. This is shown in Figure 6.3. This summary is what matters to customers to help them solve their problem. The analytics have helped us sort a list of 30 attributes and get them down to four (plus two). This gives us clarity about the POWER DRIVERS.

A brilliant everyday plain biscuit

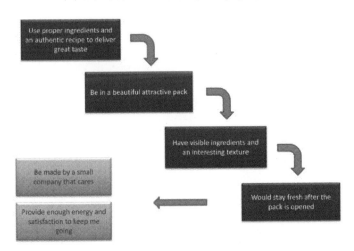

Figure 6.3 Biscuit POWER DRIVERS

Example 2: Mortgages

A study into people applying for a residential mortgage and to find out whether there was a space for mutual building societies to compete with the big banks and the old building societies that had converted to banks. This work was done in 2004 at a time when banks and building societies tended to offer better deals to new customers than to existing customers.

Here is the attribute list we developed, sorted into hot, warm, cool, cold categories. Again, this study is based on customer research; it uses the opinions of potential mortgage customers (Figure 6.4).

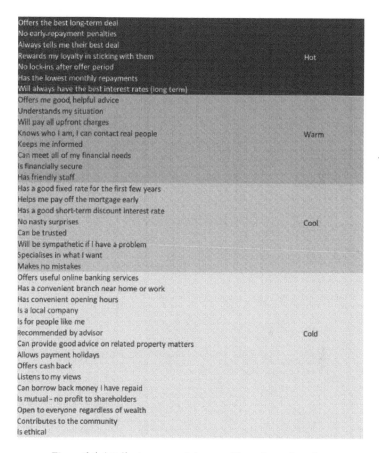

Figure 6.4 Attributes you might consider when choosing a mortgage provider

We turned this into a profile of the ideal mortgage provider using the hot attributes – see Figure 6.5.

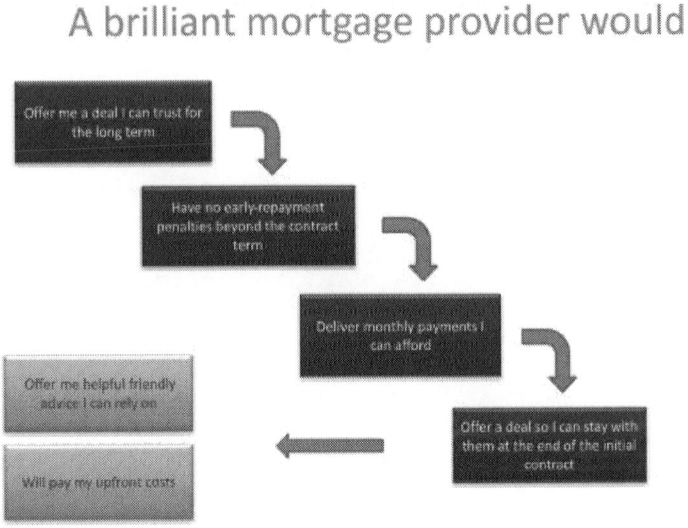

A brilliant mortgage provider would

Figure 6.5 Mortgage POWER DRIVERS

Now we have the POWER DRIVERS for potential mortgage customers. As in the PINPOINT step there are three approaches we can take to get these POSITION analytics done:

1   The intuitive entrepreneurial version: Take the attribute list and use the criteria to decide which we feel are the most important and powerful attributes for customers in choosing which to buy and pick the POWER DRIVERS out for ourselves. Then pick the attributes where we feel we compete.

2   The DIY version: Get our team together and score each of the attributes from the attribute list. We could also survey some customers or potential

customers using focus groups, interviews, conversations or online survey tools to get a measure of what is important to our customers: https://chrisradford.net/attractive-thinking/. When we have decided what the scores are then download the spreadsheet https://chrisradford.net/attractive-thinking/ where if we can insert the scores as instructed then it will give us a POWER DRIVER score for each attribute. (This does not use the proprietary algorithm mentioned in version 3 (the full version), it is a simpler calculation.)

3   The full version: Go to www.differentiate.co which explains how we can run this for you. This involves workshops with your team, customer workshops, quantitative customer research and uses proprietary analytics and algorithms developed by Joseph Khoury and Raymond Asmar from Reach Mass. The tools allow us to input the results from the customer research and get clarity. We are sure we have the right answer because this model has been tested in hundreds of markets and consistently finds that when a brand is associated with powerful attributes it has a higher market share.

We will use the POWER DRIVERS to inspire the brand positioning. What matters here is that we select the attributes that we feel will make us standout in the mind of the customer. These attributes will be the solution to the problem we described in PINPOINT.

In the next section we will look at how to create the POSITIONING STATEMENT and BRAND CORE.

Create and define our position in the market

Our analysis in POSITION has looked at a lot of functional attributes. There is a reason for this. Even though brand choices are emotionally based, when customers explain their purchase, they use rational explanations and rational language.

If you ask someone why they bought a car, they will come up with great features. It is energy efficient, fast, fun to drive, noticeably quiet and comfortable, spacious, cheap to run, etc. Whilst all these things no doubt contributed to the decision, a car is an expression of personality and there is some emotional identity that the customer must have to buy the vehicle. This simple example is a bit like the System One and System Two described by Daniel Kahneman. System One is the unconscious emotional response that drives our decision making. System Two is the slower, rational, functional decision making that we would use to justify our decision.

We start with System Two, functional and rational responses, to discover the POWER DRIVERS of decision making by customers. But once we have done this, we build an emotionally appealing brand that gets attention as well as delivering the functional benefits. We cannot develop this emotional stuff in market research, we have to do that ourselves. But we can find out about the functional stuff through market research and our own team workshops.

Let's look at a couple of frameworks we can use to build and describe a brand's positioning. But in all this work please pay most attention to the three elements of the BRAND CORE. You may have come across brand wheels, clouds, compasses, essences, pyramids and positioning statements. It is easy to get distracted by things that do not matter. There are three things that matter in the brand positioning. This is what we call the BRAND CORE:

- What we do (how we solve the problem).

- What we are known for (brand fame).

- How we leave people feeling (the brand experience).

Once we can describe these three things then we have great and simple guidance in how to develop the brand. By way of example I will illustrate these three elements using some famous brands. I have no inside track on their brand strategy. This is just how it seems to me looking in from the outside:

Coca-Cola

What do we do: Provide refreshment everywhere.

What we are known for: Coca-Cola in a red can or shaped bottle, always available.

How we leave people feeling: Refreshed.

Apple

What do we do: Create technology that is easier to use.

What we are known for: Beautifully designed technology products.

How we leave people feeling: Connected.

Amazon

What we do: Make it easier to buy anything.

What we are known for: Making buying easier.

How we leave people feeling: Unbothered.

Google

What we do: Organise the world's information.

What we are known for: Search (find what I want).

How we leave people feeling: Informed.

To write our BRAND CORE we first build the POSITIONING STATEMENT. The POSITIONING STATEMENT provides the answers to some simple questions. If we have done the work in PINPOINT and POSITION, we will find it easy:

The POSITIONING STATEMENT

Who is our customer? Who will buy this? (See PINPOINT.)

What is their problem or need that we could solve? (See PINPOINT.)

What is the actionable insight? Something about the customer's frustration or joy in the buying and consuming of the product or service that we need to constantly refer to in product design and developing our marketing message. (See your customer research.)

What do we do? (Our promise): This is what makes us stand out.

Why should the customer believe this? The emotional and rational explanation for choosing our brand. This is often four bullet points.

What are we known for? What comes to customer's mind when they think of us, what are we really famous for?

How do we leave them feeling? The emotional response when or after using the brand.

Our tone of voice: Our personality, feel and style.

Once we get this right our brand starts to feel like a person and not a thing. This defines what makes us attractive. I have prepared quite a few of these in my time and they have been done in conjunction with my clients. But this means they are also confidential; it restricts my ability to share these as examples. To create some examples, I will use two from businesses that I am involved with.

Example 1: Henry's Avalanche Talk

Who is our customer? Skiers and snowboarders who are thinking about going off-piste but are held back by a fear of the unknown. Also, skiers and snowboarders who are going off-piste but are concerned they are taking unnecessary risks.

What is their problem or need? They are not exploring all the terrain they would like and are held back by fear of the unknown.

What is the actionable insight? Avalanche awareness, snow science and mountain craft is presented as complicated and only for experts who have magical powers to stay safe. However, applying a simple checklist makes it possible to make better decisions, manage risks and enter off-piste terrain.

What we do? Help you discover that safety is freedom.

Why should the customer believe this?

- Henry is a recognised authority by media and snow sports professionals.

- Equipment manufacturer sponsorship and endorsement.

- Regular off-piste snow reports provide free information.

- Henry created the most famous and original avalanche talk in Val d'Isère.

What we are known for: The original Henry's Avalanche Talk.

How do we leave them feeling? Unleashed.

Our tone of voice: Fun, insightful, informative, reassuring.

What is the BRAND CORE? These are three central elements of the brand. These are:

What we do: Education and information for skiers who want to go off-piste but are held back by fear of the unknown.

What we are known for: Avalanche talks and snow reports.

How we leave people feeling: Unleashed.

This is the BRAND CORE and guides everything we do as a brand and a business.

Example 2: Differentiate (brand strategy consulting business)

Who is our customer? Managing directors, CEOs, business owners and marketing directors in £25m+ businesses who are ambitious for growth, willing to challenge the status quo, don't have a strong marketing team and can make the decisions.

What is their problem or need? They have had success, but growth has slowed, and they want to stimulate new growth. They understand lots about their customers but are not sure exactly what drives customers to buy. They have lots of ideas but are not sure which ones will really work.

What is the actionable insight: They know the business must innovate to achieve their goals. They believe they need to attract more customers and cannot get the growth just from selling what they have to existing customers. This requires bold action. But it is hard to win support for the big ideas that are needed to attract more customers. Getting alignment with colleagues is a challenge. They have a massive job to run the existing business, it is hard to find the time to work on big new initiatives to drive growth.

What we do? Brand strategy everyone is convinced will work.

Why should the customer believe this?

- Proven Differentiate process: Enables you to answer five business critical questions to turn insights about customers into products your customers will love, and a marketing plan you are convinced will work.

- Involves the team: Our highly inter-active workshops create insight and build ideas, but we insist you involve the wider business team, it is this that secures buy in.

- Analytics create clarity: Our propri-etary analytics tell you what really matters, know the markets where you will get growth, understand precisely why customers buy, prioritise the marketing channels that will attract customers.

- Creates new capability and skills in the team around understanding custom-ers and creating growth strategies.

What are we known for? Understanding why customers buy and creating brands that attract more customers.

How do we leave them feeling? Convinced it will work.

Our tone of voice: Supportive, enabling, knowledgeable, aha!

What is the BRAND CORE? These are three central elements of the brand. These are:

What we do: Create brand strategies that everyone is convinced will work.

What we are known for: Translating customer insight to create brands that attract more customers.

How we leave people feeling: Convinced it will work.

This is the BRAND CORE and guides everything we do as a brand and a business.

How do we produce these documents and statements? It is a tough thing to do and to get right. When we have done it, it will seem obvious and we will wonder why we had not expressed our brand so clearly before. We will also wonder why it was so hard to see before we did the hard work.

Start with the answers to the questions we developed in PINPOINT. This tells us who are our customers and what is their problem. Then use the POWER DRIVERS for guidance to develop the POSITIONING STATEMENT. Our positioning should feel like a natural and valid response to these.

It's a combination of hard graft and creativity. The best way is to run a workshop with a motivated group of people from within the business or who know our business well. A facilitator/leader who is experienced in the art will help us get a much better result. Workshop facilitators have skills that are often not really appreciated in advance of a workshop. But a skilled facilitator will help us get a much better result.

Summary

The POSITIONING STATEMENT includes the elements of the BRAND CORE. These are three central elements of the brand. These central elements that we must be able to articulate are:

1 What we do.

2 What we are known for.

3 How we leave people feeling.

This guides everything we do as a brand and a business. This is just as important in B2B as in consumer brands. If we do no other part of the positioning work, then have the answer to these three questions ready in a simple document. A few simple tips:

> *What we do:* This must be obvious and use simple language and not industry jargon. Even if we are a specialist high-end B2B service provider, our answer to this question should be easy for anyone to understand. It exists so people understand what we do.

> *What we are known for:* Be truthful with ourselves. Known for means what customers

and prospects think of when they hear our brand name.

How we leave people feeling: This is emotional, make sure we have a one-word version of this. In the case of Henry's Avalanche Talk, the word is 'unleashed'. In the case of Differentiate, the word is 'convinced'.

The PINPOINT and POSITIONING steps are often neglected when the business teams are in a hurry to get on with the next three steps:

PERFECT: Create a product or service.

PROMOTE: Communicate it to customers and prospects.

PITCH: Know how to engage all stakeholders.

But if we do the hard work in PINPOINT and POSITION then we will find the next three steps are much easier and we will develop a more effective plan. We now have clear guidance on what will attract more customers to our brand.

Chapter 7

PERFECT

How do we create a product, service or message that delivers this?

What are we trying to create?

This step is about creating and shaping what our business sells and the message we will use to explain it to customers and prospects. Through PINPOINT and POSITION, we know who we are aiming to attract, what we will do for them, the main benefits we will offer, what we will be known for and how we should leave people feeling. Now we must either create new products and services or shape our existing products and services to deliver these. We must also build a message that is attractive to customers. We are aiming here to create

- a product and/or service specification;
- the packaging;
- the message/creative idea;
- the brand story.

The *product* is the actual thing or service that solves the problem we identified in the POSITIONING STATEMENT. This should deliver the benefits described in the POSITIONING STATEMENT and some of the POWER DRIVERS we identified in the POSITION step.

The *packaging* is the physical presentation of the product or online/brochure presentation of the service. This packaging should not just be attractive and stand out, but it should convey and communicate the elements of the POSITIONING STATEMENT and the POWER DRIVERS.

The *message* is what we say about our product or service to explain it to people. This is often improved if it comes with an emotionally led creative idea rather than a dull feature-led explanation. Here are some examples of a message expressed as a creative idea:

> UL Consumer Technology – Is chosen by people who care
>
> Miracle-Gro Patch Magic – Makes patches disappear like magic
>
> Apple – Think different
>
> Pepsi (1980s/1990s) – The choice of the new generation
>
> Audi – Vorsprung durch Technik

The UL example shows a way to bring emotion into B2B technical sales. This can be really powerful as they talk about their own people and their customers' people. It connects.

The *story* is an explanation to the customer of who we are, why we do it, what drives the business team and maybe some history about the brand and the people. Most decent websites have an 'about us' page. This is where this communication naturally sits. The story is not the reason people buy from us. But there is a saying in business that people buy from people. Whilst this is not literally true every time, people do like to know who they are buying from and they want to feel good about it. A brand story helps to explain that.

The first step is to assess what we have right now and how well it is working. What we want to assess is how well each element performs at delivering our brand positioning and how well it expresses our CORE BRAND. Here is a checklist of elements of our brand that we might want to consider:

> Product performance
>
> Value for money
>
> Packaging and presentation
>
> Service delivery
>
> Brand logo
>
> Branding presence and appearance in the market
>
> Advertising materials
>
> Content for use in social media
>
> Twitter/Instagram/Facebook presence
>
> The brand story

We may have some elements of our brand to add to this list.

To assess these elements of our brand, we should get a few of us together who know something about the business and about our customers. Organise a room with each of the elements of the brand on display to act as a reminder. This could be physical products and advertising, it could be webpages, direct marketing, customer feedback. It should also include some examples of notable competitors. Then ask each person individually to give each element a score on two scales.

The first scale is to mark each of the four elements out of ten on how well they deliver the CORE BRAND:

10 = it is as good as I could possibly imagine

9

8

7 = it's good, but should be improved

6

5 = needs a lot of improvement

4

3 = this needs urgent attention

2

1 = it is absent or totally ineffective

The second scale is a seven-point scale to compare us to competitors:

7 = much better than competitors

6

5

4 = same as competitors

3

2

1 = much worse than competitors

The scores will point us to where the biggest weak-nesses are and where we should direct our efforts. Now this could lead us to decide we need to radically reap-praise our product and service offer and redevelop some-thing new to meet customer needs. Or it might tell us we just need to refine our marketing communications. Or that we need to tweak and refine some elements. The idea of the exercise is to identify which parts of our brand and business do not express the CORE BRAND today.

Now this book cannot guide each business on how to develop its products and services and how to create the PERFECT package since much of this is specific to each industry and market. However, there are some guiding principles we can follow, and I have divided these into three questions:

> What are the traps we must avoid and the tips to succeed in creating stuff?

> How can we develop creative ideas to address each of the elements?

> How do we evaluate what we have created and optimise it to ensure success?

Traps and tips in creating the product and the message

By far the biggest trap is to do exactly what our customer asks us to do. Yes, we listen to our customers about their problems and what matters to them. We have worked on a whole process designed to understand that. But the develop bit is down to us. We need to go beyond what the customer tells us and come up with ideas that they would never have imagined. Here are a few examples of things that customers would never have suggested in research and might have rejected in a concept test but have come to pass through innovation. In each case there is a customer problem that was solved by the product or service and that problem would have been discovered by customer insight work:

> *Product:* Mobile phone app to control my heating when away from home.

> *Problem:* The heating is often on when I am out, wasting money, and the house is often cold when I get in, creating discomfort.

> *Product:* The weekly delivered veg box.

> *Problem:* We are always eating the same food and getting bored with it. I would like to eat more seasonally fresh food but am not sure what is in season. I don't like shopping and/or the shops don't have what I need when I go there.

The next trap is believing that creativity is something other people do. It is tempting to think that creativity is the preserve of 'creative' people. This idea is reinforced in the creative industries and arts where there are discrete groups of people labelled as 'creatives' or 'artists'. This gives us the thought that ideas are the preserve of a separate group of people with magical creative skills. The truth of the matter is that creative talent is like all talents. It is actually hard work and practice. As Edison said, it is 1% inspiration and 99% perspiration.

Creativity is not the preserve of 'creative' or 'inspirational' people, it is about the people who are best qualified to help us come up with new ideas and those who are willing to put in the work, discipline and effort required. One of the key differentiating factors between more creative and less creative people is simply that creative people think they are creative and the less creative don't think they are.

The next trap is not having people with the right frame of mind (Figure 7.1). There are a number of creativity killers we must look out for and try to discourage team members from using them. Roger van Oech in *A Whack on the Side of the Head*[54] identified beliefs that are often embedded in the culture of an organisation. They are all legitimate in certain circumstances but invariably inhibit the creative idea-generation process. These are:

That is not logical.

There is a right answer and a wrong answer.

Don't be foolish.

That's not my area.

We must avoid ambiguity.

We must follow the rules.

We must avoid making mistakes.

---

[54] Roger van Oech (2008) *A Whack on the Side of the Head: How You Can Be More Creative*, Business Plus Imports.

Be practical.

Play is frivolous.

I am not a creative person.

Figure 7.1 Source: Marketoonist.com

There are a number of characteristics that we should look for in seeking creative help from people:

Experience of our business and our customers – great ideas that work usually come from people who know something about the products, the technology, the customers and the business.

Curiosity – a wide-ranging interest in all aspects of the world around.

Suspension of judgement – not rushing to judgement on seedling ideas.

Lack of deference – more willing to challenge authority and the status quo.

Impulse acceptance – more likely to accept unorthodox/bizarre solutions to problems.

Mental flexibility – can switch easily between ideas, a mental juggler.

Conceptual fluency – can generate lots of ideas in a short time.

Originality – comes up with unexpected solutions and ideas.

We should not assume we are not creative. Look out for creative potential in our colleagues and be wary of including people who will limit the creative process.

How do we create?

We need to create or creatively modify the four core manifestations of our brand:

- product and service;
- packaging;
- message;
- our story.

What we need is ideas on how to do things differently from the way we do them now and in a manner that will attract more customers. The POSITIONING STATEMENT and CORE BRAND guide us as to what will attract customers. What is the best way to develop ideas to execute them?

My consultancy team has worked with many of the world's leading brands and with brand training consultancies practising and teaching innovation techniques, implementing new product development processes, creative workshops and idea-generation sessions. Here is our short digest of the top lessons and techniques in how to create new ideas.

A few rules for coming up with ideas

The first rule here is that creativity does need stimulus. Now we have prepared some stimulus though the POWER DRIVERS, POSITIONING STATEMENT and BRAND CORE development work. But we should go further and try to get close to customers as part of the creative process as well. This is not asking them questions and then doing what they suggest. This is about observing what they do, how they behave and react in situations where our product or service could be relevant. Big companies spend millions on ethnographic research techniques to observe and get insights about customer behaviour. But there are other less expensive and possibly more effective methods. Here are some examples:

> Mars Petcare has cats roaming around the office and kennels outside so people look after them.

> Decathlon has its product development office attached to a store and the office staff have

to walk through the store to get to the office, they cannot enter by any other route.

Social media tracking is now widely available to see what is being discussed. There are online tracking tools for a low monthly fee or professional services to hire.

Blog posting with comments and feedback can yield insight if we post, read and listen.

The second rule is that we must try to link the logical and creative sides of the brain and use whole-brain thinking, not get stuck in just logical, practical thinking or purely hare-brained creative ideas.

The third rule may be surprising. Creativity needs rigour if it is to turn ideas into products, packaging or messages that will attract customers. Rigour is about staying in the zone of what we are doing, it is about applying the techniques as discussed below, it is about working hard on the customer insight, it is about working with what we can do and not what we can never do.

The fourth rule is that quantity leads to quality. Keep pushing out for more ideas and do not close down or evaluate too early. The activity does not have to be fast and furious. Sometimes we need to sit with the discomfort of nothing occurring for a while to give it a chance to come through. We have to kiss a lot of frogs to find our prince of an idea that can be made to work. This is part of the energy and persistence that is needed to be creative.

Some idea-generation techniques that work well

There are many techniques available; here are some that consistently work. All these techniques assume we will get together in a small group of three to eight people to create ideas. These ideas will be worked on and evaluated subsequently.

Technique 1: What's the question?

The first technique is to frame the question that we are trying to answer. It's important that everyone is clear about what we are about to address before a creative session begins. The process of clarifying what the question is can in itself be a creative trigger. The kinds of questions we will focus on when looking for ideas to make our brand more attractive to customers will be:

> *Product:* What changes can we make to solve *customer problem x,* how could we help customers solve this problem more easily?

> *Service:* How can we make it easier for customers to address *customer problem y?*

> *Packaging:* How can we make it more obvious our product delivers *power driver a?* How can we design a website or package that is more attractive?

> *Message:* What is the strap line, simple message that sums up our promise? What is an emotionally driven creative idea to communicate the *promise from our positioning?*

We should look for half a dozen ways of posing the same question differently and write them all down. We should experiment with different ways of posing the question. One person poses an initial problem/question. We check for understanding and ambiguities and come up with alternatives. Then select the question that motivates the group most. But be sure that the problem owner (person responsible) agrees that this new way of posing the question still addresses the original problem!

Then write the question down where everyone can see it during the creative session. This helps the group stay on track. Getting the question right is critical to getting the best ideas.

Technique 2: The brain dump

We simply capture all the ideas we have already had. There is a group leader who will manage the process and capture all the ideas as short phrases on a flip chart. This is not the same as brainstorming. This gives everyone the chance to put their ideas on the table. Doing this exercise frees the brain as we release our existing ideas. This creates space for new ideas.

Once the group has agreed the initial question, then everyone calls out thoughts as they occur. At the end of the session, output is reviewed. We will focus on quantity not quality and get LOTS of ideas – sifting comes later. There is no criticism allowed. The word 'but' is banned during a brain-dump session. We keep it free-wheeling; any idea is a good idea. It doesn't have to be connected to what was said previously.

If we listen to the other ideas, we will use these as a spring board for more ideas. There is no point in doing this as a group unless we actively listen and build on other ideas. We must record every idea and write everything down so we can review at the end.

Technique 3: Random word

Random word is the easiest creative technique in the book (literally). It was popularised by the inventor of lateral thinking, Edward de Bono. It can be used in groups or individually to address any situation where creativity is desired:

- Open a dictionary at a random page.

- Select the first concrete noun you see. Use this word as a stepping stone for developing an idea.

There are some rules. We always we start with the question from technique 1. But then we operate as individuals or in pairs. We will record each idea as a short phrase on a flip chart. Then we share these with the other members of the group who have done their own version and these ideas get added to the list from the brain dump.

Random means random. The word must not be pre-selected. You must take the first concrete word you see. The only exception to this is if you don't understand what the word means. The more ridiculously inappropriate the word is to the question in hand, the better.

The word is a stepping stone and not an end point. We will start with this word, and not the problem. We quickly run through what it means/looks like/sounds like/does etc. Then we can think about how these attributes might apply to the problem identified on our question. We must force ourselves to find a connection. We do not give up on a word without spending at least a couple of minutes on it. Do not start with an existing solution and work backwards to find a connection with the random word. If the connection to an existing idea is inescapable, move on to another random word.

Now we have more ideas to add to our list on the flip chart. Most people by now have had enough of idea generation and are exhausted by it. But there are some other techniques we can use to create ideas before we get on with evaluating them.

Technique 4: Contrary input

This is a way to open out the random-word technique to every element of our surroundings. It is a great discipline for individuals to develop their innate creativity. The method is to ask ourselves: What new input can I actively go out and get which I can use as a springboard for creativity? Then go get the object or experience and use it like a random word.

We need to be deliberately contrary. For example, if we are working on a specific task to, say, develop a new toothpaste, then do something different like go to a garden centre with the deliberate intention of buying three objects which have no relevance to the question. Often ideas will start to form before we have made our purchases.

If we are looking to improve our general creativity, set ourselves a goal each day to do something differently e.g. buy a different newspaper, try a new route to work etc. In the process of making these decisions and trying to execute the purchase, it will open our minds to ways of thinking we are not used to and create new ideas in our heads.

Technique 5: Sleep on it

This is proven to help us come up with a new perspective. It is a great way to both discover new ideas and to evaluate and critique the ideas we have. The notion of an idea occurring to us when we are in the shower or going to sleep in bed is not so far-fetched. New ideas form and crystallise at random moments. Creativity and ideas are not the result of a structured process (much to the frustration of large-company CEOs), they come from random stimulus encouraged by structured inputs and from concentrating on the right question.

How do we evaluate the ideas?

The simple answer is we must decide; no-one else can do it for us. Certainly, do not ask the customer to decide. It is our call and our experience will inform that judgement.

Getting from 60 ideas to 5 proposals

If confronted with a long list of ideas on a flip chart, the simplest way to reduce that down to a short list is to do a group vote. The wisdom of a group is always more powerful than the wisdom of one person. There is a simple method to capture that wisdom.

If there are 60 ideas on the flip charts and we want to have 5 of them to do more work, then issue everyone in the room with 10 sticky dots and ask them to select the 10 that they like the most. Then give them another 10 dots and ask them to select the 10 that are the easiest to implement. Count the dots. It will flush out the 5 ideas that the group in the room thinks are most appealing and most practical.

Now we work the 5 ideas up into a concept board. The best format for this is not a long-winded document describing the proposal, but a simple concept board that can be grasped by anyone in less than 15 seconds. This concept board can be created on the same day as the ideas workshop or could be follow-up work to be completed within a week.

A concept board forces us to think the idea through and express it in writing and with pictures. This creates rigour in our work. A concept board might comprise:

A title

A problem to be solved or question (optional)

A picture(s) of the product, users, situation, idea

The idea as seen by the customer

The benefits it brings to the customer

Figure 7.2 shows a simple example done in Microsoft PowerPoint.

Evergreen spray and feed

Simply attach the bottle to your hosepipe.

Use spray nozzle to direct the water onto your lawn.

The fertiliser is applied automatically.

Greens your lawn in 24 hours.

Figure 7.2 Example of concept board

Figure 7.3 is an example designed professionally.

Figure 7.3 Example of a concept board

There is an art to writing these and we can get brand design agencies to do it for us, but we can also just do them ourselves with a pen and flip chart or using Power-Point slides and images we can find online.

Sifting the proposals/concept boards

The temptation here is to go and ask the customer to rate the concept board and tell us if they would buy it or not. We should not do that. Since customers are unable to predict their behaviour in the future, the answers they give to these questions are not reliable predictors. Market research firms offer all sorts of techniques and promises that they have made their methodology reliable. Then when their predictions do not come to pass, they will say that their client did not execute the same thing that was researched so that is why the result was different. But whilst that may be true, it still says that there was no point in doing the concept testing with customers.

The only reliable way to get customer feedback is to ask them to buy it if it is a product or packaging, or to run the advertising or marketing campaign and see the response if it is marketing communications. We need to get the real thing in front of customers and ask them to act and then observe their behaviour. So how do we choose which concepts to develop into a prototype or test market?

Instead of using concept testing with customers we can create our own list of criteria to help us choose which we should develop and take to market or test market. Here is a list of criteria to assess any product, service or packing idea, improvement or any creative execution to deliver a marketing message to our customers. Score each concept board or idea on each of these criteria:

Criteria list

How well does it help customers solve a critical problem?

How well does it deliver/communicate a POWER DRIVER?

How consistent is it with our POSITIONING STATEMENT and BRAND CORE?

Can we afford it? Does the cost make sense?

Can the customer afford the price we must charge?

How easy is it for us to execute and deliver this?

Can we do this quickly and in a timely manner?

Use a ten-point scale to do the scoring for each of the criteria:

> 10 = it is as good as I could possibly imagine/completely affordable
>
> 9
>
> 8
>
> 7 = it's good, but should be improved
>
> 6
>
> 5 = needs a lot of improvement
>
> 4
>
> 3 = this needs urgent attention
>
> 2
>
> 1 = it is absent/totally ineffective/will not work/too expensive

We should start by assessing our ideas using these criteria on these scales and do this ourselves. We could then go on to do customer research on our concepts using the same questions and the same criteria. Unlike the 'will you buy it?' question, this is a question customers can answer. We can expect answers from customers that reflect how they think and feel about our ideas. They are just reacting to what they see. They are not predicting whether they will buy. This feedback can help us make modifications.

Prototype and test marketing

What we do need to do is to get the product, service, packaging or message in front of customers and measure their behavioural response. Do they buy, do they notice us, do they change their beliefs about our brand? In some markets this is difficult, in some this is much easier, but we must try to find a way that works for us. To help us think about this I have listed some examples.

Minimum viable product: Eric Ries in *The Lean Startup* introduced this idea.[55] This was initially aimed at software and tech products, the point being to create the minimum functionality that would work for a customer and put in on sale. This will cause us to learn and we may choose to pivot our business in a different direction as a result of the experience of making some sales to some customers. My clients Leigh Ashton and Jonathan Mills at Sasudi discovered this as they developed a sales training platform for small business owners. After six months of being on sale, they pivoted and created a customised version of their sales training platform aimed at larger businesses with bigger sales teams. However, the underlying tech and method of their training remained and proved to be very valuable.[56]

Sell in a few shops: Many food start-ups (e.g. Innocent Drinks) start by selling on market stalls, in specialist stores or via subscription websites to get some direct customer reaction before investing in the manufacturing and distribution systems required to scale up.

Use limited affordable media: Get marketing ideas out first using an affordable media such as social media, Google Ads or direct marketing to see what effects we can measure. This may not be direct sales, it may be changes in awareness and attitude, but get a customer reaction by putting it out there in a real environment.

---

[55] http://theleanstartup.com/Eric Ries
[56] www.sasudi.com/; www.sales-consultancy.com/

If we cannot do a real test market, then we should get some customer reaction, but do not use market research techniques, do it ourselves, show friends and family, put it out on social media to a select number of customers, have some private conversations with customers and get a reaction. But we should do this ourselves and listen to the feedback rather than take what they say literally.

Now in larger corporations the C-suite executives will demand a market test of some sort before making any significant investment. The best way is to test a minimum viable product in a real test market. However, it may be that we cannot deliver a minimum viable product to test market. This means we would have to use a market research test.

For this research we must develop amazingly realistic concept presentations in concept boards, 3D physical product or video. Then we can use the market research to find out how well our product, packaging, service or message delivers on the POWER DRIVERS that we discovered in POSITION. We know that if customers see our product or service delivers those POWER DRIVERS then it is highly likely the customers who have the problem that we are solving will go and buy the product. We can conclude that if our product is seen to deliver the POWER DRIVERS then the customer will buy it. This insight is more powerful for us than the simple answer to the question 'will they buy it?'.

Create our brand story

Think of this as the 'about us' page on the website. Every business should have one; it is where we tell the customer and prospect about who we are, where we come from, why we do what we do. It helps people to connect with us and our brand. It will never be the reason they buy from us, but it will help them feel connected to us.

We like to get to know people before we spend too much time with them. It is the same with brands: Customers like to feel comfortable with a brand before they buy.

A story influences the emotional relationship with the brand. This kind of story is most evident when a founder shares their story. But it can work with larger brands who express their story and purpose as a brand. Dove talks about being the home of real beauty and working to make beauty a source of confidence, not anxiety. UL talks about working to make the world a safer place. Henry's Avalanche Talk aims to liberate all skiers to explore more of the mountain, have more fun and stay safe.

How do we write our story?

It already exists. We just need to discover it. It is in the heads of the people working in and on the business and the founders. We must go round and interview some people who work in the business covering a variety of roles and different levels in the organisation. If we can find eight people to do it, that is enough. If there are fewer than eight in the business, then talk to everyone. Conduct a 30-minute interview with each of them asking some questions:

> How did the business get started? What was the original idea behind the business?

> What really matters to our customers about what we do?

> What is it like to work here? How would you describe the culture?

Are there some values that guide the business team and influence how we work here?

What gives you a buzz each day when you work here?

What frustrates you about working here?

This will provoke a discussion that flows and brings out different aspects of the brand and the business. We can then turn this into a story. Here is an example of one for a caterer to large businesses.

Staying one step ahead

From small beginnings...
Like every business, we started with an idea. In 1936, our founder sold fresh food from the boot of his car to busy workers passing by. But he quickly saw he could provide a better service by putting vending machines in factories and offices – these were places they had never been before. This was because, for him, the business was not just about selling food... it was about innovative thinking and great customer service. From that first day of trading to the team we are today, we are still united by those same core beliefs.

Just for you...
When it comes to delivering in-house catering, providing good quality, delicious food at an affordable price is the challenge that most companies face day-in, day-out. Cost efficiency

often results in standard programmes and a lack of real innovation follows. We believe we need to stay one-step-ahead to keep our restaurants busy and profitable, so we create individual programmes for our clients and keep new ideas flowing for the guests.

Listening harder...
We create better solutions by listening harder and in more ways. As well as regular customer and guest surveys, we run customer work-shops. These keep us on our toes and the feed-back we get is directly translated into dishes, new menus and into improving our service and creating new service ideas.

All about ideas...
We have a culture where new ideas are encour-aged and rewarded. For example, our teams researched the best ketchup recipes and developed our own premium ketchup brand for our clients. We encourage our chefs to enter awards, so they get recognition for their hard work. We work hard to attract great chefs; we train them and give them freedom to work hand-in-hand with our clients. Some have even won national awards. But all our chefs can be front-of-house making sure they understand who they are cooking for and listening to feed-back first-hand. They can confidently create their own menus; we provide menu software that prices every item. This helps chefs stay creative and our restaurants remain profitable.

Staying one step ahead...
By listening harder, attracting the best chefs, providing cutting-edge systems and constantly innovating, we and all our clients stay one step ahead. We have come a long way since 1936, winning many awards, but we remain committed to be a fresh-thinking company, just as we were in those early days.

Guten Appetit!

This format works for a brand story. It is primarily an internal document that guides us and all the business team and any agencies about who we are, why we do what we do, what our values are and how we behave as a brand. The elements included in the story were:

> The history
>
> What matters to customers
>
> How we deliver against that
>
> The things we do to stand out with customers

We also went on to specify:

> The underlying truths about the business, the brand and the team:
>
>> We promise a culture where people are valued and can make a difference
>>
>> We attract and invest in great chefs
>>
>> We listen more and in different ways, to deliver better service and more relevant innovation

We are big enough to deliver and small enough to care

Brand guidance on what the brand is and what it is not e.g.:

We are: *One step ahead of guests*

We are not: *Running to catch up with what you want*

We do: *Leave you on top of things*

We do not: *Leave you overwhelmed by issues*

Our chefs are: *Listening to you*

Our chefs are not: *Telling you what to eat and when*

Our chefs are: *Visible and available*

Our chefs are not: *Hidden in the kitchen*

An even better way to express this to the team is to make a video. Some video examples of this that we have done at Differentiate have brought the business team to tears as they see their hard work and effort come alive. Video is emotional. You can see two examples of these company and brand story videos for UL[57] and Litmans[58] . Video conveys emotion more powerfully than text.

When we have done the internal communications and shared the documents and materials with our team, then we can create a customer facing 'about us' page on our

---

[57] https://vimeo.com/120598109
[58] https://vimeo.com/204859453

website and incorporate this in our brochures and other marketing materials. Here is an example of this kind of 'about us' story as presented to customers on Henry's Avalanche Talk website:

> Henry's Avalanche Talk (HAT) provides training and essential information for skiers who want to go off-piste but are held back by fear of the unknown. HAT is known for helping ordinary skiers have an extraordinary experience off-piste. We aim to leave people feeling liberated and unleashed.
>
> Henry's Avalanche Talk (HAT) was founded by Henry Schniewind. HAT has been around for 25 years and grown into a team of off-piste professionals. We have given talks and courses to tens of thousands of people, presented at international snow science conferences and published many papers and articles, often in the British press.
>
> There are two types of skiers we help. The first are experienced skiers who go off-piste, take risks they don't understand and could easily suffer an avalanche accident. The second are regular skiers who are reluctant to go off-piste because they think it is dangerous and scary due to avalanche danger and the hazards of navigating unfamiliar terrain.
>
> But avalanche accidents are not random unpredictable events. It is a fact that 9 out of 10 avalanche victims trigger the avalanche themselves. This means that once you know how to manage the risks, you can make the off-piste no riskier than

driving your car at home. The conventional solution is to hire a guide, but they are expensive and are often reluctant to share their knowledge. If people do look up professional avalanche literature it tends to reinforce the idea that this stuff is too difficult to learn and that off-piste remains off limits, dangerous and scary.

We have created a method that demystifies the expertise and teaches skiers how they can go beyond the piste, have much more fun and stay safe, all at the same time. The programme helps people answer the critical question 'Is it safe out there?' We explain that there is no simple yes or no answer. The right answer is it depends on you. It depends on where you go and when, how you go down or up and how well prepared you are.

We deliver training in the UK, Val d'Isère and online. HAT is known for helping ordinary skiers have an extraordinary experience off-piste. We aim to leave people feeling liberated and unleashed.

Summary

PERFECT is about creating and shaping what our business sells and the message we will use to explain it to customers and prospects. Through PINPOINT and POSITION, we discovered who we are aiming to attract, what we will do for them, the main benefits we will offer and what we will be known for. In PERFECT, we created new products and services or shaped our existing products and services to deliver these things. We also built a message that is attractive to customers. We must create:

- a product and/or service specification;
- the packaging;
- the message/creative idea;
- the brand story.

Be careful how we involve the customer in this process. We must not ask them if they will buy it and believe their answer. This is the same for B2B and consumer brands. In B2B we need a product to offer (a product can be a package of services), we need design and packaging that presents our brand and makes it recognisable, we need a creative idea to convey our core message and we will be much more attractive to clients with a great brand story.

The subjects behind PERFECT that I have covered here are the content of many separate books. Some of them require years of experience to refine. But everyone in business does them for better or for worse. I have tried to provide some techniques that can be used by anyone and highlight the hazards and traps where we might go wrong.

The next step is to let our customers and prospects know about it.

Chapter 8

PROMOTE

How do customers find out about it and where do they buy it?

Let them know about it and make it easy to buy

The task here is to do what Byron Sharp called creating mental availability and physical availability. Once we have created something (PERFECT) that solves a problem for people or addresses their needs (PINPOINT) and we have found a way to communicate that (POSITION) then we do not need to resort to clever tricks and devious persuasive marketing. We already built persuasiveness into the product, the positioning and packaging. What we need to do is: *Let them know about it and make it easy to buy.* This is what marketing is. Keep it simple. In this chapter about PROMOTE, we will look at an organised process to figure out the best way to achieve this simple goal.

We start with a quick recap of the rules of customer behaviour and the principles of effective marketing communications. This sets up the first part of the process, which is to select and agree the priority marketing tasks that we must deliver to attract more customers. We go on to look at how we should communicate with our customers and choose the marketing channels that will work best for us. Then a brief review of the tricky question of how much should we spend on marketing and the wisdom of seeking expert advice.

Recap the rules of customer behaviour and the principles of effective marketing communication

Here is a recap of some rules of customer behaviour and some principles of marketing communications that we looked at in Chapter 3.

Rules of customer behaviour

Rule 1: Many more customers buy bigger brands than buy smaller brands and they buy bigger brands slightly more often than they buy smaller brands.

Rule 2: Customer loyalty is a mirage, customers are not 'loyal' in an emotional sense. They have habits. They buy our brand for as long as it suits them, when they stop buying it is either because they don't need it any more or they found an alternative that is more suited to their needs.

Rule 3: Brand reputation is firstly what drives customers to buy and will determine our profitability and underpin our growth.

Rule 4: Short-term sales activation effects are only short term.

Rule 5: Brand building investment is essential to create long-term brand value and profit.

Principles of effective marketing communications

To grow we must attract more customers; we must increase our market penetration. The IPA study showed that the most effective campaigns always had increasing market penetration (not loyalty) as their primary goal. This must be the focus of our marketing activity.

There is a direct relationship between brand awareness and future brand sales. If awareness is going up and we have an attractive product, then sales will go up. If awareness is going down then regardless of the product and service, sales will go down.

There is a huge risk of customers simply forgetting about us as they go about the hurly burly of their lives. We need to create brands that are memorable, well branded, easy to recall, easy to remember the name, and provide continuous reminders.

Figure 8.1 illustrates the work done by Benet and Field on short-term sales activation vs long-term brand building campaigns. We can see in the sales graph that after a short-term activation campaign, the sales boost is large but the sales return to the level they were at before the campaign. There is no long-term effect. Whereas with long-term brand building campaigns the immediate sales boost is smaller but the effect lasts much longer and the base level of brand sales builds over time.

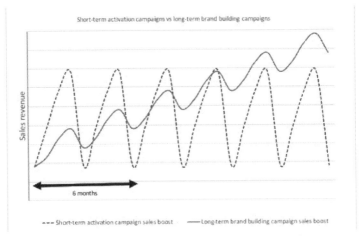

Figure 8.1 Illustration of how the sales effect differs in short term activation campaigns vs long term brand building campaigns

The most effective campaigns split their activities 60:40 in favour of emotionally driven branded communications (Figure 8.2). Emotionally driven branded communications are really those that build our reputation. Direct sales activities stimulate customer purchases.

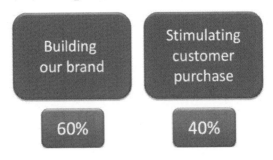

Figure 8.2 How to split marketing investment

Now when we are considering which marketing channels and marketing methods work to do each of these tasks, it helps to break down the tasks into more detail. Figure 8.3 shows a useful way to break down the tasks.

Marketing tasks

Building our brand	Stimulating customer purchase
Being front of mind	Stimulate trial
This is the kind of brand I will like	Recapture lapsed users
Help learn about the brand benefits	Encourage brand choice vs competitors
Makes me feel the brand will help me	Increase usage and frequency

Figure 8.3 Detail on the different marketing tasks

Building the brand (emotional) is about four marketing tasks:

1   We start with awareness and being front of the customer's mind because without that we do not even get considered. This comes from having memorable brand icons and frequent exposure to them. By brand icons I mean logos, colours, advertising ideas, jingles, etc.

2   Then we need to create familiarity and likability. This usually comes about from multiple experiences

and interactions with the brand. It is the same as when we meet people, the first time we meet them we are not sure about them but as we meet them more often, we become more comfortable. We must find a way for people to experience the brand or experience our brand communications several times before they will trust us.

3 Then people need to understand the benefits that the brand will bring them, how it helps them solve a problem. This could be via website, advertising, social media, email or face-to-face sales meetings.

4 Finally, and most difficult to know how to do, is to become a brand that people understand is for them. This involves being great for customers, having an attractive story, being relevant to their problem, having the right tone of voice.

Stimulating customer purchase is also about four marketing tasks:

1 Encouraging and stimulating trial with sampling, offers to try, introductory offers. The goal here is to get people to try, to give them an experience of us. This requires advertising and reaching out beyond our existing customers.

2 Incentives to bring back lapsed users. This could be special offers or could be just communicating with them in a targeted way through email lists and social media rather than offering price reductions.

3   Encouraging choice vs competitors is about higher visibility, better display, better position in search engines, higher awareness, short-term offers and emphasising our advantages.

4   Increasing usage and frequency. This is often little more than reminding people we exist. They can easily forget about us. (Do not try to buy loyalty and frequency – it is an expensive way to do marketing with poor long-term results.)

Creating an effective marketing campaign to promote the brand requires us to decide three things:

1   Determine which of these marketing tasks we should address as a priority.

2   Know which marketing channels are best suited to the marketing tasks. By marketing channel, I mean *any way that conveys an impression of our brand or business service or triggers a behaviour towards that brand.*

3   Determine the mix of investment in marketing channels that will attract more customers short term and long term and meet our immediate objectives.

Determine which marketing tasks or objectives we should address as a priority

In the previous section we looked at marketing tasks. We need to make some choices about which of these we should invest in. They were under two headings:

Build the emotional affinity with the brand

Awareness and being front of the customer's mind

Familiarity and likability

Understand the benefits that the brand delivers

Be a brand for me

Stimulate prospects and customers to buy

Encouraging and stimulating trial

Bring back lapsed users

Encouraging choice vs competitors

Increasing usage and frequency

For most businesses most of the time the biggest opportunity is awareness, trial and bringing back lapsed users (Chapter 2). This can be hard to grasp when we work in a business. In our lives the brand lives with us every day. We know that many prospects have not yet heard of our brand. But emotionally we feel as though everyone we meet must have heard of our brand.

My business partner Henry Schniewind experiences this. He knows we have an awareness problem at Henry's Avalanche Talk. But as he lives in Val d'Isère where many people have heard of us and he is sought out by the media as a commentator on avalanche accidents and issues, then in his world it can feel like we have good awareness. Henry has to keep reminding himself there are many people who have not heard of Henry's Avalanche Talk.

Getting more customers should be the primary goal of our marketing campaigns. Binet and Field's analysis of over 1,000 IPA effectiveness awards entries shows that campaigns that set increased market penetration (more customers) as the goal outperform campaigns that set increased customer loyalty as the goal. This sample is biased to larger well-known brands. Smaller brands have an even bigger job in order to create awareness and trial.

We have come across marketing and sales funnels as a tool and a system to attract and convert customers. These tools are built to ensure we address each of the marketing and sales objectives separately at different stages of the customer journey. Whilst many sales funnels are pitched as extracting the most from customers, the structure of them is based on addressing a sequence of marketing tasks that make sense to attract customers. A sales funnel starts with the goal to secure more trial. It is a numbers game with some brutal attrition of numbers from the first goal to the last goal:

For consulting services

Awareness – 1,000 people aware (awareness)

Understanding – 20 willing to take up the first offer to find out more (familiarity, likability, understanding)

Experience – 5 willing to engage with the first experience of the brand (is it for me)

Sales – 3 sign up for the product

For consumer products (in store or online)

Awareness – 10,000 people aware

Understanding – 3,000 go on to learn more or get a recommendation from friends

Experience – 500 actually visit the store and see the product

Sales – 50 pick it up this month.

Once we know these numbers for our business it tells us how many people we must make aware and then follow up with to generate more sales. The first marketing task is to get awareness amongst many thousands of people.

The next tasks after awareness are to build familiarity, likability and understanding of what we offer. This process will involve marketing communications in advertising and marketing channels, but it is likely to involve trying something to get an initial experience of the brand. It is only with an initial experience that we can really get our prospects to understand what we offer. The best way is to create some 'trial products or experiences'; these maybe given away for free or sold at low cost. Here are some examples.

Key Person of Influence approach

Daniel Priestley in the Key Person of Influence programme advocates a product ecosystem as the best way to make more sales. The products feed each other. If we are selling personal or business services, we might consider any number of these types of products:[59]

- *Free:* Information or services that prospects can access for free (not even requiring an email address) to create awareness of what we offer and credibility that we have expertise e.g. blogs, videos, articles.

---

[59] Daniel Priestley (2014) *Key Person of Influence,* Rethink Press.

- *Advice:* More detailed help that is offered in exchange for personal data such as email and telephone; this might be a scorecard, a test, an online seminar.

- *Trial product:* Something people pay for that gives prospects real value and experience of what we offer e.g. a book or a workshop event.

- *Sales event:* A strategy session that a prospect pays for that is directly valuable and allows us to ask for a sale.

- *Full and complete solution:* Our core product or service at full price e.g. training event, software installation, consultancy delivery, coaching service.

- *Follow up:* Something that offers value to customers of the core product after they have consumed the product or service.

Having these different products in the product ecosystem focuses the marketing and selling task to create awareness and trial of each product in the ecosystem. The product ecosystem allows us to make requests to prospects that are easy for them to accept at the start and then move onto pitching the core product later:

> Read some free information or watch my free videos
>
> Then
>
> Try out our scorecard test or invest time with us in webinars
>
> Then

Come to our event, read my book

Then

Tell us something about you in our strategy session, get some customised advice

Then

Buy the core product!

Then

Here is how you can stay in touch

At each point in the process these are small steps and the prospect is ready for them. If the prospect is not ready for the step, then they probably are not going to buy the core product and they will fall away from the process. The prospect may choose to jump some steps.

This product ecosystem is superior to a sales funnel; it is the Attractive Thinking version. It attracts with products that offer value; it does not extract. This can be applied in different ways in all markets. The underlying thought here is to take each of the marketing objectives and then think of what we can create that will deliver value to the customer and achieve this objective. Here are two examples addressing each of the objectives:

Squires Garden Centres (retail)

Awareness: Create visible retail sites, local press articles, local press advertising.

Familiarity and likability: Their on-site cafe is the biggest and most powerful trial product that gets people to experience the store.

Understanding: Events programme from training, talks, workshops, Santa Claus, advice centres in-store, local advertising and direct mail of seasonal offers.

Brand for me: All the above.

Encouraging and stimulating trial: In-store display, customer advisors, special offers.

Bring back lapsed users: Promote the cafe.

Encouraging choice vs competitors: The service.

Increasing usage and frequency: All the above.

Miracle-Gro (consumer brand)

Awareness: TV advertising.

Familiarity and likability: TV advertising.

Understanding: TV advertising, website, packaging, in-store advice.

Brand for me: Product technology and packaging design is for a specific type of gardener who wants convenience and ease and is willing to pay a bit more for something that helps.

Encouraging and stimulating trial: In-store display, retail special offers, local print advertising.

Bring back lapsed users: New products and TV advertising.

Encouraging choice vs competitors: Keep awareness up via TV and in-store display, product innovation via technology investment, maintain packaging advantage delivering convenience.

Increasing usage and frequency: Launch new products that help in further areas of the garden e.g. water-retaining compost, Patch Magic Grass Seed, dispensing systems.

We must consider that addressing each of these eight marketing tasks is often delivered by product creation and innovation alongside marketing communications. If we have a product ecosystem designed to address each marketing task, then the marketing plan must generate awareness and trial of each of the products in the ecosystem. We may choose to advertise our events, our scorecard, our cafe as well as our brand benefits and our core offer.

Know which marketing channels are best suited to the marketing tasks

A marketing plan involves choosing the right marketing channels. We start by creating a full list of all candidate channels. By channel we mean *any way that conveys an impression of our brand or business service or triggers a behaviour towards that brand.* The process for developing this list is much the same as attributes development in POSITION. Sit down round a table in a small group and write down everything we can think of that does this. We can list them on a flip chart or use sticky notes to gather our thoughts. Figure 8.4 shows an example of a channel list developed through a sticky notes exercise.

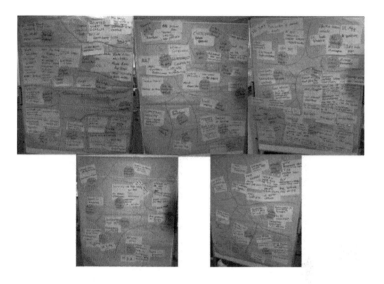

Figure 8.4 Example of channel list developed in a workshop

And here is the full list. This example is from a B2B service business:

Attend our own events

Be in paid-for industry directories

Be in the accrediting body directory

Be in trade magazines

Email and info to business unit managers in our organisation

Email newsletter updates

Exhibit at trade shows

Face-to-face meetings with prospects and customers

Google AdWords

Hire sales agents

Industry event sponsorship

Meetings with business unit managers in our organisation

Organic search in Google

Our online service chat lines

Our website

Participate in industry working groups

Read customer testimonials

Recommendation by people who know

Ringing up customers/prospects

Send a personal email

Sharing our knowledge in articles/blogs

Speak at industry events

Trade association events

Work with partner organisations/partnerships

Here is another example channel list developed for a consumer brand in food and drink:

Ads on buses and taxis

Articles in magazines

Available in places I go to eat out

Available in places I like to spend leisure time (e.g. cinemas)

Back of pack information

Billboards

Branded website

Cause-related activity (e.g. charities)

Celebrity endorsement

Character (e.g. cartoon) endorsement

Cinema ads

Coupons from store loyalty scheme

Coupons in newspapers or magazines

Drunk by family/friends/relatives

Exclusive distribution in an outlet where no competitor products are on sale

Flyers in magazines and newspapers

Free items or gifts with purchase

Google Display ads

Facebook ads

YouTube advertising

Magazine ads

On pack promotion (e.g. instant win, limited editions)

Packaging design and colours

Posters

Price reductions

Product displays in shops

Product placement in TV programs or films

Product sold from a chiller cabinet or fridge

Radio ads

Recommendation of family member

Recommendation of friends

Sampling in shopping centres or on the street

Sampling inside shops

Signs on the shop shelf about promotions or prices

Signs outside shop

Sponsorship of music events

Sponsorship of sports events

Sponsorship of TV programs

TV ads

Volume price promotions (e.g. buy one get one free)

The point of this exercise is to consider all the options before we make choices about which are the right channels. I urge you not to leap on the latest fad or choose something because it worked for someone else. The task here is to focus on awareness and trial and to end up with a programme that is 60% invested in building our emotional brand and our reputation and 40% invested in stimulating immediate and quick sales.

Determine the mix of investment in marketing channels that will attract more customers

From this long list we need to create two short lists. The first list is our preferred channels that will build the emotional brand and our reputation. The second list is our preferred channels that will drive direct and immediate sales. We need to deploy these channels using the 60:40 budget split. There are several ways to create a short list with differing levels of investment in our time and money.

The intuitive version: Take a stab at it and pick out the five channels that we think are the best suited to the tasks of building brand reputation and stimulating immediate sales. This is instinct and judgement using our beliefs and experience (or even prejudices). Even though this is basic, it is quick and at least we considered all the options before making our choices.

The DIY version: This is where we use a scoring matrix. There is an example you can download at https://chrisradford.net/attractive-thinking/. In this case we give a score to each channel on how well it delivers the marketing task. The scale is a seven-point scale like this:

7 = as well as any channel, very effective

6

5

4 = is OK at this but others may be better

3

2

1 = does not do this well at all

This allows us to create a ranking for which channels do each of the two tasks the best. It is based on our judgement. But if we do the exercise involving a small group and combine everybody's individual scores, this will be a more refined guess than we achieved in option 1.

We might have different tasks and objectives for each of the products in the product ecosystem since they are each designed for different groups:

> New prospects, have not heard of us
>
> New prospects, have not bought before
>
> Have bought before, but lapsed
>
> Are current customers but have not bought everything yet
>
> Have tried our trial product but not bought the core product

The tool allows for this and helps us create a priority channel list for each of the products in our product ecosystem based on which type of prospects or customers they are aimed at. Here is an example of the B2B priority channel list for each of the main tasks:

Building the brand and reputation

Our events programme

Exhibit at trade events

Speak at industry events

Website/organic search

AdWords and YouTube

Thought leadership – blog, webinar, email

Stimulating short-term sales

Ringing up customers/prospects

Direct mail/email offers and reminders

Meeting prospects face to face

Have a referral scheme for clients

Meet other business unit managers in our business

Here is an example of priority channels for consumer products:

Building the brand and reputation

TV ads

Drunk by family/friends/etc.

Recommendation of family and friends

Magazine articles

Cinema ads

Stimulate short-term sales

Price reductions

Available in cafes and leisure places

Sampling in shops

Coupons (newspaper/magazine)

Product displays

I have found this answer is not untypical for many consumer products in many categories.

Note that price reductions are 'effective' and may be essential based on the retailer demands but can be very damaging to profits and usually are not worthwhile. The biggest issue is that price reductions will be 'given away' to customers who are already convinced of the brand and its benefits, so we give away a lot of profit vs the number of new customers it attracts. Further to that, new customers attracted by lower prices may not come back to us when our product is at normal price. Whilst the model indicates price reductions are powerful, try everything else first.

The full version: There is a way to consult with consumers on the effectiveness of each marketing channel and to turn their observations into a channel selection tool. The tool is called ICOM (Integrated Communication Measurement), Joseph Khoury of Reach Mass devised it.[60] It uses all these principles and involves a large consumer survey and some modelling tools. It also provides a budget calculator for what is needed to have a market impact and how to optimise the allocation of funds to marketing channels. It is expensive but powerful for big brands with marketing budgets over £5m. It is the only truly independent tool to allocate budgets to marketing channels. Take a look at www.differentiate.co to find out more about how to access this tool.

Use an external agency: Give an external expert agency all our insights, marketing strategy, brand strategy and objectives, explain your thinking and have them recommend. But there are issues with this, since most agencies specialise in specific channels and are not best equipped to choose between all the channels. (See section on using agency specialists later in this chapter.)

---

[60] http://reachmass.com/icom-integrated-communication-mea surement/

Some observations on specific channel choices

Is it true that nobody watches TV anymore/TV advertising is a waste of money?

Our own experience might suggest this is true. Gary Vaynerchuk promotes this theory as he built his media empire using Facebook and content marketing strategies. But it is not true; people are still watching live TV. Mark Ritson explains why Gary Vaynerchuk is wrong.[61] Thinkbox TV publishes evidence that people still watch TV.[62]

There are big differences in people's receptiveness to advertising depending on where it is shown. When people are online, they are frequently in 'task mode' or 'active mode' and less susceptible to interruptions and other messages. When they are watching TV, they are in passive mode and ready to receive, observe and remember.

TV has the biggest reach of any single medium. It is the one that engages the greatest range of senses using vision, motion, sound, drama to get the emotional response. TV is the medium that delivers that emotional type of advertising we need not just to create awareness but to create a longer term emotional affinity that we need to build the long-term response. TV is one way (not the only way) that still works to get that awareness and build the brand.

---

[61] www.marketingweek.com/2018/11/16/mark-ritson-gary-vayn erchuk/

[62] www.thinkbox.tv/Research/Thinkbox-research/The-Age-of-Television-the-needs-that-drive-us

Byron Sharp and Andrew Ehrenberg's work showed us how easy it is for us to forget about a brand, even a brand that we buy from time to time (Figure 8.5). TV-advertised brands have higher awareness and are easier to recall.[63]

Figure 8.5 Source: Marketoonist.com

Les Binet and Peter Field show us how to make TV work. TV still has the biggest reach and it still has the powerful engagement and impact on customers.[64]

Is TV advertising too expensive for us?

TV advertising is not an efficient way for many businesses to reach niche or discrete markets, so for many businesses it is simply not the right choice. TV may have the best

---

[63] Bryon Sharp (2010) *How Brands Grow: What Marketers Don't Know,* Oxford University Press.

[64] Les Binet and Peter Field (2018) *Effectiveness in Context,* IPA.

reach for consumer products with a wide appeal, but the entry cost for a TV campaign is £250k and is more likely £2m to £10m. What do we do?

First of all, if we are considering spending £250k on marketing then we can speak with some agencies about TV and alternatives. For example, TVLowCost runs a specialist service to provide TV advertising for small businesses. Andrew Mitchell has reworked all the costs of media and production to create TV campaigns for £250k.[65]

Is digital marketing the thing that works best?

The channel list exercise showed us all the channels that might work. There are likely to be some digital marketing options in the list. But we should be careful of the distinction between digital marketing and marketing. It is an unhelpful and misleading distinction. Mark Ritson argues that the digital distinction is redundant. It is better to think about digital channels rather than digital marketing. Digital marketing is a subset of all the types of marketing that are available to us.[66]

The IPA study shows us that many companies are over investing in digital marketing. Digital channels are now receiving a higher share of spend than their share of impacts. As a result, it is becoming an expensive channel and marketing budgets are being spent less effectively than previously.[67]

There are many other offline ways people find out about things. Their family and friends tell them, they see things in shops, they read about them in newspapers and

---

[65] www.tvlowcost.co.uk/

[66] www.marketingweek.com/2019/02/20/mark-ritson-shut-down-digital-marketing-teams/

[67] Les Binet and Peter Field (2018) *Effectiveness in Context*, IPA.

magazines. They see things advertised at events. They go to exhibitions and events. There are billboards.

The IPA study also shows us that digital is better at stimulating immediate short-term sales than it is at building long-term brand reputation, so it can seem attractive, but digital over-investment leads us to spend more than 40% of our investment in short-term sales activation. This means our budget is not optimally deployed.[68]

Digital marketing channels can be immensely powerful. But please let's not exclude the other options. Let's look at our channel choice from the point of view of the customer not the point of view of the medium we want to use. Let's consider all the channels.

Partnerships are powerful

This is my absolute favourite marketing channel for smaller (and larger!) businesses. This is partnering with a brand that is already in contact with our potential customers and using their network to reach our prospects. The question we need to ask ourselves is: *Which brands or organisations who are in touch with our prospects have a problem that we could solve?*

Partnerships arise when two organisations launch a programme that benefits both parties. This is the marketing strategy at Henry's Avalanche Talk. Mountain sports retailer Ellis Brigham hosts talks and promotes Henry's Avalanche Talk events to its customer base. This provides Henry's Avalanche Talk with venues and promotion and provides Ellis Brigham with a point of difference. Ski Club GB provides promotion for the events in return for discounted tickets for its members and the

---

[68] Les Binet and Peter Field (2018) *Effectiveness in Context*, IPA.

opportunity to be promoted in the talks. Safety equipment and sportswear manufacturer Ortovox want to reach the Henry's Avalanche Talk audience and provide sponsorship funding in return for promotion at the training and the talks and lend Henry's Avalanche Talk some credibility. This is a cocktail of partnerships.

Start listing organisations that are in touch with our customer base and then we can think of some ideas for what problems they might have that we could help them with. This helps us prepare a pitch and a conversation with them.

Social media can be powerful but is limited

We have heard people say that social media offers potential for free marketing and advertising and is easy to do by picking up a mobile phone. It seems ideal for small business owners. We can create a Facebook page (or even a group), we can tweet, we can blog, we can post on LinkedIn or Instagram and we will reach an audience. We may be able to build up a large following for our brand.

Our primary marketing task is to generate awareness and trial amongst new prospects and convert them to customers. The problem with our social media lists and followers is that they are people who have already heard about us and at least know of the brand. They are also our most engaged and enthusiastic followers. This does not mean we should not do it. It does mean that what we are doing is engaging with our existing customers and lapsed customers and people who already have heard of us. The social media channels are particularly good at staying connected and following up; they do not work so well to draw in new prospects.

It is noticeable that the most successful people using social media build their followers and fan base using other media than social media. They recruit followers at live events, by writing in other media, by appearing on TV. The Kardashian social media following exists because of the TV programme. Business speakers and leaders recruit followers by speaking and publishing elsewhere e.g. Tim Harford, the economist and journalist, Robert Peston, the journalist.

The numbers of followers and engaged fans are insufficient to meet our marketing goals. This is especially true as the business gets bigger: 6,000, 10,000 or even 50,000 is often just not enough people. If that is enough to meet our awareness target, then the channel may work.

Paying for advertising and posts in social media is advertising, it is not social media

Facebook advertising, YouTube advertising, Google Ads, LinkedIn, Instagram Ads are the brand leaders in this field. These are powerful tools and can be used in campaigns for both brand building and short-term sales activation. The data these companies hold about their user base make them enormously powerful at targeting. Using these advertising tools is a sure fire way to reach new customers. We must look at them carefully and find someone to help who knows what they are doing.

Distribution, availability and easy to buy matters

The reason Coca-Cola is the biggest selling soft drink in the world is not the famous brand and the advertising; it is because it is available for sale (and chilled) in more places than any other drink. Whenever I have looked at what are the most effective promotion channels for a food and drink consumer brand, availability is always one of the top five channels.

The reason Amazon is the fastest growing retailer in the world is because it is the easiest to use; it makes buying easier than any other website.

Byron Sharp describes the marketer's task as one of creating mental availability and physical availability for our brand. This enables customers to buy:

- Mental availability is being in the mind at the time the need or problem arises (awareness). This is better promoted by having brand icons, images, logos, jingles, advertising that are easily recalled and recognised.

- Physical availability means being available in more places, easy to find and easy to buy.

What are some methods used in other markets to become easy to find and easy to buy?

Number of shops where we are distributed

Being promoted and stocked by distributors in our market

Visibility within the shop, how easy is it to find

Appearing in search engine results

Online businesses being referenced and promoted in offline media

Frequent appearances in advertising so prospects are reminded

Easy to use shopping cart

Fast checkout

Easy to book (hotels, restaurants, travel tickets)

How much should we spend on marketing?

Only we can decide. There is not a right or wrong answer. Back in the nineteenth century in the USA, John Wanamaker proclaimed: 'Half the money I spend on advertising is wasted; the trouble is, I don't know which half.'

Marketing and advertising experts will try to convince clients they can be more efficient than that. Digital marketing and programmatic advertising hold out promises of greater efficiency through targeting techniques and tracking results and conversions. This measurability can dramatically improve the performance of sales activation campaigns.

But given the work by Binet, Field, Ehrenberg and Sharp we also know that we need to build brand reputation and create an emotional connection with our audience. This is 60% of our budget and is much harder to measure exactly how, when and what works. The 40% we spend on sales activation needs this brand investment if it is to work.

Putting up a big display of products in a supermarket with a compelling price offer will still struggle to get many sales if no-one has heard of or trusts the product. We must still make a brand building budget and fear that 50% of it is not working. There are a few other rules that can help us create a budget.

Share of voice drives market share

Those who spend more, create more awareness, reach more people, stimulate more reminders, reach more lapsed users and create greater salience. This means that share of voice is an excellent predictor of what will happen to market share in the following few months. Studies by research companies and consultancies show this to be true time and time again. Nielsen, Millward Brown, McKinsey and Kantar have all measured this effect. The academics that I referenced in this book (Binet, Field, Sharp, Ehrenberg) have also shown it. It is an empirically proven law of marketing. There is also a database of company performances called PIMs (Profit Impact of Market Strategy); this database has benchmark data from over 4,200 firms and reached the same conclusion. Share of voice drives market share (and market share drives profit success).[69]

The first guiding principle in setting a budget is to match our marketing spend with our market share objective. One will follow the other. This is one of the reasons that companies who invest in marketing spend during a recession come out of the recession much more strongly than those who don't. What happens is those who cut back the marketing spend lost share of voice, those who maintain their spend get an extra benefit because their share of voice increases.

If we cannot afford the share of voice we need to hit our market share goal, then we must review our sales target and market share objective. We cannot defy this rule.

How much can we afford?

Broadly and regardless of the market we are in, if we do not spend between 5% and 10% of net sales value on marketing we will struggle to maintain and grow the number of customers. This may not be enough if we are

---

[69] www.malik-management.com/malik-solutions/malik-tools-and-methods/pims-profit-impact-of-market-strategy/

launching something new and creating a new brand. Sometimes new launches will spend up to 50% or even 100% of first-year revenues to get started. The share of voice argument then tells us what we can expect to get for that. This percentage spend is just on marketing and sales support, but excludes our headcount spend on marketers and sales people.

The Attractive Thinking approach

However much we can afford to spend on marketing, if we develop products, services and messages that are more attractive to customers, add value for them and solve a real customer problem for them, then marketing and selling will be easy, since all marketing has to do is *let them know about it and make it easy to buy*.

The use of agency specialists

We must do this. We must find agency specialists to help us or we will waste a lot of money. The skills are specialist and we need help. Finding the right agency for us is hard. The main issue here is that media and advertising agencies tend to specialise in specific media, so they are not best placed to advise us on which media to use, they have a bias. Digital marketing specialists will use digital, Facebook marketers will use Facebook, big advertising agencies like TV and broadcast media.

What this means is that we must brief them with our view of the marketing plan. If we do the exercises outlined in this book, this will equip us to make decisions about the channel mix and it will help us to brief the agencies.

The agency may well come back with a different perspective. We should listen and adapt based on what they say but remember we are deciding what the channel mix is. The agency's job is to execute that and the budget as effectively as possible. But if we show up with...

> Our customer research
>
> Our brand POSITION STATEMENT
>
> Our BRAND CORE
>
> Our BRAND STORY
>
> Our PERFECT messages and any creative ideas
>
> Our PROMOTE plan and channel mix

...then they will be able to do a much better job. They may want to amend some of our thinking and our plans. We should listen, but we must argue for what we believe is right and stick to it. After all it is our brand and not theirs.

Summary

In this chapter we have looked at how to focus on this simple marketing task: *Let them know about it and make it easy to buy.* Doing this requires us to consider eight tasks under two headings. We need to invest 60% in the brand building and 40% in the sales activation:

Build the emotional affinity with the brand

Awareness and being front of the customer's mind

Familiarity and likeability

Understand the benefits that the brand delivers

Be a brand for me

Stimulate prospects and customers to buy

Encouraging and stimulating trial

Bring back lapsed users.

Encouraging choice vs competitors

Increasing usage and frequency

We must consider all the channels that influence and reach our customers and prospects and select a short list of five channels for each of the headings. Don't get sucked into the fashion for digital advertising, look at it from the customer's point of view:

- Remember people are still watching TV.

- TV may not cost as much as you think.

- Facebook advertising is not 'social media'; it is advertising and can be immensely powerful.

- Look at the evidence and be guided in the budget by the share of voice argument.

- B2B requires the same discipline and thinking. The channels may be different but this approach is the same as for consumer brands.

- Hire an agency or agencies to help with executing the strategy.

Chapter 9

PITCH

How do we engage our shareholders, board directors, colleagues and customers?

Engaging everyone is essential for our plan to work

Every five years or so there are articles written about why marketers are not more respected and why their influence on the business is not as great as it should be (according to marketers). This subject has been studied by The Marketing Society, by the *Harvard Business Review*, by McKinsey and many others.[70]

---

[70] www.campaignlive.co.uk/article/marketers-lack-influence-board room/776449?src_site=brandrepublic;
www.emrrecruitment.co.uk /blogs/marketers-lack-boardroom-influence–31752415195;
www.marketingweek.com/2015/09/30/why-marketers-are-fail ing-to-get-a-place-in-the-boardroom/;

The themes that come up are the same ones that have been around for a long time. As each generation of marketers arrives, they come up against the same struggle to engage the business team in their mission. Between 1996 and 2000, my consultancy firm SYNESIS did some work in conjunction with The Marketing Forum, the HR Forum and the Finance Directors' Forum to look at this issue. We also came across some academic work by Elliot Maltz of Williamette University looking into why firms are more or less market orientated and how effective marketers are in helping a business be market orientated.[71] Our SYNESIS work included surveys and discussion groups amongst 300 marketing directors and managers and 200 directors and managers from other functions in 100 different firms. This work revealed insights into the problem faced by marketers in winning support for their plans.

The relationship between marketers and finance and other functions was poor in most firms. Marketers typically had a higher opinion of their impact and effectiveness than did the people in other functions they worked with. However, marketers were often respected for specific skills they had with quotes like this:

---

www.marketingsociety.com/the-library/how-marketers-need-raise-their-game;

https://hbr.org/2004/11/bringing-customers-into-the-board room;

www.mckinsey.com/business-functions/marketing-and-sales/our-insights/engaging-boards-on-the-future-of-marketing

[71] Elliot Maltz (1997) An enhanced framework for improving cooperation between marketing and other functions: the differential role of integrating mechanisms, *Journal of Market Focused Management* 2, 1, 83–98.

Marketers are...

Bright... creative... arrogant... young... ambitious... vibrant... professional... They are the most intelligent and qualified in the business.

But this was tempered by a concern:

They tend to prefer the glitz to the graft. They tend to focus externally i.e. going to see the agencies, rather than getting down to the factory. They tend not to be as commercially strong as I think marketing people should be.

The finance directors described the marketers' lack of commercial sense:

brash... wide boys... flash... uncontrollable... into freebies... bored by numbers... never in the office... over enthusiastic...

HR saw the marketers working in isolation and not communicating with the business:

they sometimes make decisions in isolation, believing they know best about the brand... they should be more communicative, less purist, more pragmatic and less egotistical.

A better marketing team and marketers would be like this:

The only successful marketing teams are where people can look at the business as a whole.

The work of Elliot Maltz and colleagues examined the things that made firms more market orientated and how marketing influence worked in the boardroom.[72] One of their observations was that marketing teams in the firms that are most market and customer orientated spent more time within the business talking with other functions in the business than marketers in those firms that were less market orientated who spent less time talking to their colleagues and more time focused externally with customers and agencies.

This complemented our SYNESIS finding that marketers were often seen as spending too much time with their agencies and not enough time in the business. Marketers develop a good understanding of customers, but not enough understanding of how the business can act to respond to customer needs. Marketers also do not have good relations with others in the business and this restricts their ability to win support for their ideas. The problem is not the marketer's expertise in their field, it is their ability to win support for their proposals and translate the insight into something that the business can realistically deliver.

What this means for us as creators, marketers and CEOs is that we must not only come with a plan to attract more customers that we are convinced will work, but also we must get a plan that everyone is convinced will work.

This is the holy grail for creators of brand strategy. Attractive Thinking aims to create a brand strategy that everyone is convinced will work. Shareholders are

---

[72] Elliot Maltz, William E. Souder and Ajith Kumar (2001) Influencing R&D/marketing organizational integration and the exchange of information between R&D and marketing parties, *Journal of Business Research*, 52, 69–82.

convinced that the future value of their shares is in good hands. Board directors are convinced they are doing their best to attract more customers and to do that in a profitable way to maximise returns for shareholders. They understand they are engaged in a worthwhile endeavour to help customers rather than exploit them. The team in the business are convinced their work is worthwhile; they are helping people to solve a problem. This engenders a culture of helping each other as well as helping customers. Customers' experience of our brand is positive and rewarding, they will come back for more. This is a virtuous circle of reinforcement as all stakeholders in the business and brand have a good experience and reinforce each other.

This is different from the environment of an extractive strategy focused on making the most money from customers and maximising short-term profits. In this scenario, shareholders will like the quick rewards but be worried whether the long-term value will be there. Board directors are consumed by cost cutting, profit margins and getting the most from their customers rather than how they help the customer solve a problem or address a need. Staff end up focusing on 'what is in it for me?', which does not create a great internal culture. Customers have a transactional feeling about the brand and feel a bit exploited. No-one really feels it is working well.

We have followed the steps outlined in PINPOINT, POSITION, PERFECT and PROMOTE. Now our strategy will be easy to write. We write down the answers to these four Attractive Thinking questions:

1   Who are our customers and what are their problems?

2   How we can solve those problems and stand out?

3 How do we create the product and service that delivers this?

4 How do customers find out about it and where do they buy it?

We write our answers on a few sheets of paper and keep it short, in plain language and easy to understand. This makes it easier to explain to others.

Explaining it to others is the essence of this chapter. We can only engage our shareholders, board directors, colleagues and customers if we have a compelling way to communicate the strategy. Every time we do this, we are pitching the strategy. A compelling pitch offers something attractive and beneficial to the other person, easy to understand. This is how to pitch our brand and our ideas to improve the brand. If we acquire this skill, we will not only have a brand strategy to attract more customers, but also we will have one that everyone is convinced will work.

There are two different approaches that stand out as being more powerful ways to help us PITCH our ideas. They work in two different situations:

1 Pitching to someone who does not know us and/ or does not know about the brand, the business and what it does. This requires us to answer the questions 'What do you do?', 'Why should I invest?' or 'Why should I buy?'

2 Pitching internally to someone who is engaged with the business, but we need to explain an idea we have and make a request for them to help us. This could be pitching the board for investment, asking for support from the sales or production

team, getting our marketing agency to do something for us, persuading the web developers to take on a project, etc.

Pitching externally

This is one of the least taught and potentially most valuable skills for anyone who wants to create a brand strategy and attract more customers. Rather than invent my own approach, the method I will share here is called Perfect Pitch and is taught by Mike Harris who used this to pitch for and create businesses that went on to sell for millions. His company Mercury Communications became Virgin Media, his First Direct banking is still the bank with the best customer service, his Egg Card was sold to Barclaycard and his Garlik internet security company was sold to Experian.[73] This method makes pitching seem easy and simple, but like all simple things, it is hard to get right and takes a lot of practice.

We introduce our brand or business by going through a series of steps:

> *Clarity:* Our name, what kind of thing we do, what categories we operate in.

> *Credibility:* Evidence of why we are any good at this, why a customer should take any notice.

---

[73] Mike Harris (2008) *Find Your Lightbulb,* Capstone; www.iconicshift. co.uk

Problem: What is the customer need or problem that we are trying to solve, where is the gap in the market?

Solution: How we solve it, what we offer.

Reputation: What we are known for.

Brand experience: How we leave people feeling.

This helps people know exactly what we do and whether it relates to them or not. Then we can go on to explain our current situation: What is happening right now, what I am engaged in, and make a request: What help do I need, what am I looking for.

Clarity

This is a statement that allows people to pigeon hole us as a person or our business in a category. People must get it immediately. This is not where we differentiate ourselves. This is where we help people get clear. Some examples:

Differentiate are brand consultants helping CEOs and marketers create strategies that everyone is convinced will work.

Henry's Avalanche Talk provides training and information for skiers who want to go off-piste but feel held back.

Maxwellia is a new Pharma company building a pipeline of new consumer healthcare brands by converting prescription only medicines (POM) to versions that can be bought in a pharmacy or supermarket.

Credibility

This is an easy reference of why we are good at this, it is a reason people should listen to us. This should be short. We are trying to get rid of the question that is in the listener's head. If they have not heard of us, then they are thinking: Who are these people? Are they any good? Some examples:

I was a marketing director at Pepsi and launched a consultancy working with leading consumer brands for 25 years from Mars, Scotts Miracle-Gro and high-end B2B services.

Henry's Avalanche Talk created the original avalanche talk in Val d'Isère in 1990 and has given avalanche talks to hundreds of thousands of skiers ever since. Henry is a sought after commentator by the national media to discuss avalanche accidents and mountain safety.

Maxwellia are the UK and EU experts in switching. The team has a unique combination of medical, pharmacy, regulatory and branding skills drawn from GSK, Boots, J&J, Boehringer and was involved with switching Ella One, Zantac and Imodium.

Problem

This comes from our POSITIONING STATEMENT for example:

> *Differentiate:* Marketers and CEOs can find it difficult to engage the whole business team in the need to invest in long-term brand building as well as short-term profits, yet this is essential to attract more customers. Businesses are also often overloaded with data and insights about their customers but struggle to get clarity on what it all means. Often the team is unclear what really drives customers to buy or not buy. Without this clarity it is hard to create a brand that attracts more customers.

> *Henry's Avalanche Talk:* There are two types of skiers we help. The first are experienced skiers who go off-piste, take risks they don't understand and could easily suffer an avalanche accident. The second are regular skiers who are reluctant to go off-piste because they think it is dangerous due to avalanche danger and the hazards of navigating unfamiliar terrain.

> *Maxwellia:* We have noticed that there are a growing number of people who suffer annoying lifestyle-limiting conditions, who want to manage their health without bothering the doctor but they are unable to access the medicines and information they need because they don't have time, don't understand what is wrong or the best drugs are

only available on prescription. Despite this, the established pharmaceutical companies are often reluctant to switch their medicines either because they lack the skills or believe a switch will be too expensive to deliver or are concerned about cannibalising their existing POM business at a lower margin. Whereas consumers want to treat themselves without the need to visit the doctor.

Solution

This is our answer to the problem. Again, this will be written into the POSITIONING STATEMENT. We have explained clearly who we are and what we do, why we are credible at this and what the problem is. Now we turn all that around and start to differentiate ourselves and stand out with our solution:

> *Differentiate:* We have evidence on why customers buy and how they behave. Business leaders can discover how this works for them using our five-step process to get clarity on what matters to customers and turn that insight into products, services and messages that will attract more customers. This involves the business team, is free of marketing jargon and ensures the CEO and marketer have a strategy that everyone is convinced will work.

> *Henry's Avalanche Talk:* We have created a method that demystifies the expertise and teaches skiers how they can go off-piste, have much more fun and stay safe. The

programme helps people answer the critical question 'Is it safe out there?' We explain that there is no simple yes or no answer. The right answer is it depends on you. It depends on where you go and when, how you go down or up and how well prepared you are. We have turned these questions into a checklist that skiers can use to make going skiing off-piste no more dangerous than driving to the ski resort.

Maxwellia: Our team has developed a method to improve the way medicines can succeed in the reclassification process and then ensure they are designed and commercialised. This is called the Dynamic Switch™ process. This makes switching a medicine from prescription only to being sold over the counter simpler, faster, cheaper and more likely to succeed.

Reputation and brand experience

This comes from the BRAND CORE and POSITIONING STATEMENT. It is what we are known for and how we leave people feeling:

Differentiate is known for understanding the POWER DRIVERS that attract customers and leave people feeling convinced the plan will work.

Henry's Avalanche Talk is known for its avalanche talks and snow reports and leaving people feeling unleashed to have more fun.

> Maxwellia is known for making medicines more widely available and leaves people feeling in control of their health.

I have now put one of these pitches together to see the flow.

An example of a complete pitch

> Maxwellia is a new Pharma company building a pipeline of new consumer healthcare brands by converting prescription only medicines (POM) to versions that can be bought in a pharmacy or supermarket.

> Maxwellia are the UK and EU experts in switching. The team has a unique combination of medical, pharmacy, regulatory and branding skills drawn from GSK, Boots, J&J, Boehringer and was involved with switching Ella One, Zantac and Imodium.

> We have noticed that there are a growing number of people who suffer annoying lifestyle limiting conditions, who want to manage their health without bothering the doctor but they are unable to access the medicines and information they need; because they don't have time, don't understand what is wrong or the best drugs are only available on prescription.

> Despite this, the established pharmaceutical companies are often reluctant to switch their medicines either because they lack the skills or believe

a switch will be too expensive to deliver or are concerned about cannibalising their existing POM business at a lower margin. Whereas consumers want to treat themselves without the need to visit the doctor.

We have developed a new method to improve the way medicines can be reclassified and then how they are designed and commercialised. This is called the Dynamic Switch™ process. This makes switching a medicine from prescription only to being sold over the counter simpler, faster, cheaper and more likely to succeed.

Maxwellia is known for making medicines more widely available and leaves people feeling in control of their health.

Once this is conveyed, we are in a position to say what is going on right now, where we have got to, what we want to do next and make a request.

How to do this?

Get a few of the team together armed with all our answers to the first four questions in our brand strategy and work out the pitch wording in a short workshop. Then we go practise it and try it out on people to see what reaction we get, and whether it makes sense. This PITCH will develop over time. What we need to do is hold this structure and these answers in our heads. Then all the content is at our fingertips and we are ready to answer that question: *What do you do?*

Once we are happy with it, then we can put it on our website in the 'about us' section. We should start training the business team to use it. Print it out, frame it and put it on the walls. It will make it so much easier for all the team to answer the questions: What do you do? What does your organisation do? Everyone will be better ambassadors for the brand. They will also become convinced our brand strategy will work.

Pitching internally

We go up to someone with what we think is a great idea and explain to them and then we find they disagree or do not like it. We are then deflated, annoyed, puzzled and this holds us back. This has happened to me often.

Then I met a director at Pepsi called Ross Lovelock. He has developed a complete and effective answer to this problem. It was originally based on processes that we were trained and required to use at Pepsi to pitch for our plans and budgets. But since then Ross has turned this technique into a whole training and strategy consulting tool called SCQuARE. I will share a glimpse into this in this chapter. But you can read more about this in Ross's book, *The One Thing You Need to Know*.[74] In his book Ross shows how to develop this pitching approach and how to turn it into a strategic planning tool to make better decisions.

The real focus here is to create a pitch or proposal that wins support. SCQuARE is an acronym and stands for:

> *Start point and setting:* Start with where we are now, something we both agree on.

[74] Ross Lovelock (2013) *The One Thing You Need to Know,* John Wiley.

Changes, complications, causes and consequences: Highlight what has changed since we started.

Question: Define the pivotal question that we must address as a result.

Answer: So what we must do is…

Recommendation: Our next steps to get this done are…

Evidence: …and this is why we should be confident it will work.

Like the Perfect Pitch as taught by Mike Harris, Ross Lovelock addresses the psychology of the recipient by dealing with the questions that are in their heads as we talk our way through it. In the case of the external pitch, start with clarity on what we do. In the case of the internal pitch, this is not necessary. The person knows what the business is. But we do need to create a different kind of clarity.

Here is a very brief summary of the approach to this kind of internal pitch. I would recommend reading the book to get the full detail on this. It is a skill that takes time and practise to acquire. I show an example of the approach here.

Start point and setting

We open the discussion with a statement that achieves two things. First to clarify what kind of subject or area we want to discuss. Second to open with something that we both agree upon. We start our pitch in a manner where we are both nodding our heads in agreement. We will start with a statement that is structured like this:

State what the project is e.g. I would like to talk about our CRM implementation.

Then describe the aim of the project e.g. we want our teams to provide a much more personalised response to our customers and do this with less cost to us and more quickly for the customer.

Then say what is working well e.g. we have done a sweep of potential suppliers and found a solution that meets our original goals.

Finally, summarise the desired outcome e.g. so we can meet the deadline in the project plan.

We have engaged the person we want to pitch to, clarified what we are talking about and now we are both moving in the same direction. If they disagree with any of this, we should stop. If they do not support the project and disagree with our aims, then they are unlikely to support the rest of the discussion. But this should not happen.

Changes, complications, causes and consequences

Now we are in a position to introduce new information that our pitch target may not have fully appreciated. This is usually that something has changed that means we will not achieve our stated aim. For example:

But the EU has announced new GDPR legislation that will require us to have higher security on the system and provides significant constraints on who we can communicate with. It means we need more explicit consent from the customer before we communicate.

Question

This is the pivot point in the pitch. Getting this right or wrong will determine if our pitch succeeds or fails. The question we ask will lead to the solution. Our solution is the answer to the question. In our CRM example:

The question we are facing is how can we create this personalised communication and still save our staff time, yet comply with these new requirements?

Answer

This is the answer to the question. It has been set up by the Start point, the Complication and the Question. This frames the debate about whether this is the right answer because now we are just discussing possible answers to the question and not a whole host of other ideas. For example:

This means we will need a higher level package from the CRM provider or we will need to look at different options; this could have implications on cost or timing.

Recommendation

These are the next steps to deliver the answer and thus to deliver our strategy. For example:

> I am pulling together a revised proposal including the impact on budgets and timings. It is likely that we will either have to put back the date of launch or experience a higher cost.

Evidence

These are some reasons to believe that the answer and the recommendations will work. This could be our previous experience, an endorsement, a competitor action. For example:

> But the team are right behind this and believe they can work with either option to get a CRM that will deliver and be cost-effective for us.

Preparing our SCQuARE pitch requires us to think through our approach more rigorously. The process will help us produce a better answer than the one we started out with and enable us to engage people and get commitment to what we are trying to accomplish.

Summary

In this chapter we have explored how to get a strategy that everyone is convinced will work. This is about engaging the business.

First, we must listen to and communicate with our colleagues across the business. The research shows that marketers who spent more time internally with other teams, as well as their own team, to learn what the business can do and communicate the brand and marketing plan are more successful at helping the business be market- and customer-led rather than supplier-led.

Second, that as we go through the five-step process, we must involve people from finance, operations, R&D, sales and HR in our workshops and planning sessions. They will bring valuable insights and feel much more committed to the plan. It creates credibility for the whole-brand strategy and business plan.

Third, that we should develop a PITCH that explains our business to any external person. We should practise this and use it whenever we are asked: What do you do? If we can get the wider business team to learn this pitch and use it in their conversations, they will be better ambassadors for the company, and they will feel a greater sense of belonging. It really helps people if they can explain the value of what they do.

Fourth, that there are internal pitching skills which really help us get support from other people in the business. The SCQuARE approach is an excellent method. But whichever method we use, we should pay attention to how we pitch and explain our ideas internally.

Chapter 10

Conclusion

A brand strategy that everyone is convinced will work

The analysis in this book together with the five-step programme is my answer to this challenge that we must not only come up with a plan to attract more customers, but also we must get a plan that everyone is convinced will work.

Underlying all of this is an approach to developing a brand strategy that involves the whole business team. The critical factors for success in doing this came out of the SYNESIS research in 2002. Marketers and creators who can get the business to invest in brand building and focus on attracting more customers are doing three things all at the same time:

1   Understand and champion the customer cause throughout the business.

2   Speak in the language of the business. Bridge the language gap between that which P&L speak and business goals require, and the things marketers talk about.

3   Create an environment for dialogue and involvement with colleagues.

The best CEOs do this all the time. It is their leadership style. The Attractive Thinking approach makes this job a lot easier. We:

- focus on attracting more customers not extracting more from the customers we already have;

- agree that our purpose in business is to help our customers solve a problem or address a need;

- start with and understand the customer in depth;

- understand unconscious biases;

- know that the future is impossible to predict, randomness and black swan events will overrule;

- know that customers find it easy to forget about us and we are not that important really;

- are wary of common sense and look for evidence and science.

We have a five-step process to create a brand that will attract more customers. This quite simply avoids marketing jargon and creates the answers to five questions:

1   Who are our customers and what are their problems?

2   How can we solve their problems and stand out?

3   How do we create a product or service that delivers this?

4   How do customers find out about it and where do they buy it?

5   How do we engage our shareholders, board directors, colleagues and customers?

I set out in the introduction that I am aiming to bring lessons from the world of big business, entrepreneurs and small business and make them accessible to anyone trying to create and manage brands. You do not need big budgets or large teams to take this approach. More money helps but it is not the only key to success. The approach is rooted in how people behave and what drives their decisions to buy or not buy.

Attractive Thinking is designed to make our brand and our organisation not just stronger but 'antifragile'. We can respond to external events. By answering the five questions in the five steps called PINPOINT, POSITION, PERFECT, PROMOTE and PITCH, we build an organisation and brand that is focused on helping customers solve a problem and address a need. This is essentially dynamic and responsive to customers. Our reputation and ability becomes grounded in solving that problem rather than delivering one product, one technology or one service. Our purpose is to help customers solve that problem. This purpose is core to our brand and our organisation.

Continue the conversation

If you got this far in reading the book, this subject must engage you. You can follow my posts on this in the Attractive Thinking blog at www.chrisradford.net. You will also find more resources at https://chrisradford. net/attractive-thinking/ to you help implement the approaches outlined in PINPOINT, POSITION, PERFECT, PROMOTE and PITCH.

If you want to join a discussion in a closed, safe space with people of like minds and see what others think about these questions and the approach to Attractive Thinking, then please join the Attractive Thinking Facebook group. This is what Facebook call a secret group, the group and the posts are not visible to anyone outside the group. It is a place to discuss experiences of trying to implement these strategies and learn from others. If you want to do this, then sign up at https://chrisradford.net/attractive-thinking/ and you can get the link to join by email.

Further reading and useful websites

The role of purpose and the need to focus on creating value for customers before shareholders:

James C. Collins and Jerry I. Porras (1994) *Built to Last: Successful Habits of Visionary Companies*, Random House.

John Mackey (2014) *Conscious Capitalism*, Harvard Business Review Press.

Commentary on many aspects of marketing and the importance of value creation:

www.marketingsociety.com/ – a global membership organisation comprising marketers and CEOs.

www.marketingweek.com/focus/mark-ritson/ – Mark Ritson in Marketing Week.

Eric Ries (2011) *The Lean Startup*, Crown Publishing.

The rules of customer behaviour and why attracting more customers is critical:

Byron Sharp (2010) *How Brands Grow: What Marketers Don't Know*, Oxford University Press.

Jenni Romaniuk and Byron Sharp (2015) *How Brands Grow: Part 2: Emerging Markets, Services, Durables, New and Luxury Brands*, Oxford University Press.

Les Binet and Peter Field (2007) *Marketing in the Era of Accountability*, IPA.

Les Binet and Peter Field (2013) *The Long and the Short of It*, IPA.

Les Binet and Peter Field (2017) *Media in Focus: Marketing Effectiveness in the Digital Era*, IPA.

Les Binet and Peter Field (2018) *Effectiveness in Context*, IPA.

Byron Sharp (2012) *Marketing: Theory, Evidence, Practice*, Oxford University Press.

The role of randomness, unpredictable events and the need to become 'antifragile':

Nassim Nicholas Taleb (2007) *Fooled by Randomness: The Hidden Role of Chance in Life and in the Markets*, Penguin.

Nassim Nicholas Taleb (2008) *The Black Swan: The Impact of the Highly Improbable*, Penguin.

Nassim Nicholas Taleb (2012) *Antifragile: Things that Gain from Disorder*, Penguin.

How unconscious bias works, why we should not rely on common sense:

Daniel Kahneman (2011) *Thinking, Fast and Slow*, Farrar, Straus and Giroux.

https://en.wikipedia.org/wiki/List_of_cognitive_biases

Richard Shotton (2018) *The Choice Factory*, Harriman House.

Duncan Watts (2011) *Everything Is Obvious*: *Once You Know the Answer: How Common Sense Fails Us*, Crown Business.

James Surowiecki (2004) *Wisdom of Crowds*, Doubleday; Anchor.

Positioning a brand to stand out:

Al Ries and Jack Trout (2001) *Positioning: The Battle for Your Mind*, McGraw Hill.

Jack Trout (2001) *Differentiate or Die, Survival in Our Era of Killer Competition*, Wiley and Sons.

Roger van Oech (2008) *A Whack on the Side of the Head: How You Can Be More Creative*, Business Plus Imports.

Creating a product ecosystem and becoming oversubscribed:
Daniel Priestley (2014) *Key Person of Influence*, Rethink Press.
Daniel Priestley (2015) *Oversubscribed*, Capstone.

Why share of voice matters and how to get on TV:
www.tvlowcost.co.uk/
www.thinkbox.tv/Research
www.malik-management.com/malik-solutions/malik-tools-and-methods/pims-profit-impact-of-market-strategy/

Creating a business strategy and pitching it to win:
Mike Harris (2008) *Find Your Lightbulb*, Capstone.
Ross Lovelock (2013) *The One Thing You Need to Know*, John Wiley.

Printed in Great
Britain
by Amazon

32115014R00160